COMES THE DAWN

LEONARD E. READ

COMES THE DAWN

The Foundation for Economic Education, Inc.
Irvington-on-Hudson, New York 10533
1976

THE AUTHOR AND PUBLISHER

Leonard E. Read has been president of The Foundation for Economic Education since it was organized in 1946.

The Foundation is a nonpolitical, nonprofit, educational institution. Its senior staff and numerous writers are students as well as teachers of the free market, private ownership, limited government rationale. Sample copies of the Foundation's monthly study journal, *The Freeman,* are available on request.

Published October 1976

ISBN-O-910614-57-1

To
Those who look into the perfect law,
the law of liberty, and persevere, be-
ing no hearers that forget, but doers
that act.

HAVE FAITH!

Faith makes the discords of the present the harmonies of the future.

—Collyer

As the flower is before the fruit, so is faith before good works.

—Whately

Faith is to believe, on the word of God, what we do not see, and its reward is to see and enjoy what we believe.

—Augustine

Strike from mankind the principle of faith, and men would have no more history than a flock of sheep.

—Bulwer

All I have teaches me to trust the Creator for all I have not seen.

—Emerson

Epochs of faith, are epochs of fruitfulness; but epochs of unbelief, however glittering, are barren of all permanent good.

—Goethe

CONTENTS

1. COMES THE DAWN   1

   Faith in freedom will allow it to burst forth and
   overcome the darkness of socialism.

2. LIFE'S GREATEST OCCUPATION   8

   Trying each day to surpass yesterday's self is to
   lead a full and useful life.

3. THE HERITAGE WE OWE OUR CHILDREN   17

   Let us preserve and bequeath to coming generations the foundations of liberty we inherited.

4. OUR PROBLEMS: BLESSINGS IN DISGUISE   23

   Growth—and happiness—consist of problems
   overcome.

5. THE ROLE OF DIFFERENCES   27

   Each of us is unique and the whole case for liberty hinges on our differences.

6. TWO DIRECTIONS AT ONCE   36

Out of a mass movement toward socialism
emerges a growing countermovement for freedom.

7. PRE-EMPTORS: AGENTS OF DESTRUCTION   45

Pre-emption of any activity by government curbs
the creative effort of individuals.

8. THE VAGARIES OF VALUE JUDGMENTS   53

Let us carefully examine an idea rather than worship or malign its bearer.

9. IDLE WORDS   58

Actions speak louder than words, and self-im-
provement is the key to a better society.

10. ARE YOU OUT OF YOUR MIND?   63

That person is out of his mind who uses or advocates coercion to get his way.

11. HERDED, OR HEADED ONE'S OWN WAY? 69

Let each pursue his creative uniqueness, rather than force him into a common mould.

12. HOW MEASURE GROWTH? 74

The GNP affords no useful measure of the growth—or failure—of the individual or business unit.

13. IDOLIZING ERROR 81

Nothing is more harmful to freedom, a brand new truth, than slavery, an error as old as mankind.

14. FREEDOM TO CHOOSE—BUT WHAT? 87

Choose only that which is good; never that which is evil.

15. PROMISES MEN DO AND DO NOT LIVE BY 93

By each man's performance may his promises be judged.

16. THE CASE FOR SEEKING 99

No one knows more than a millionth of one per cent of anything!

17. AM I A PART OF THE PROBLEM? 103

If you are not a part of the solution, you are a part of the problem.

18. WHERE LOOK FOR OUR EMANCIPATORS? 108

He best serves others who most thoroughly attends to his own business.

19. LET'S LOOK TO OUR PRINCIPLES 115

If it's right in principle, it has to work.

20. THE CHARITABLE ECONOMIST 120

Let not him who is houseless pull down the house of another.

21. THE GOOD LIFE: A FLOWING ACTION 125

Learning is life's most enjoyable experience—
at once a growing and flowing action.

22. THE WONDER OF WONDERS 131

The world will never starve for the want of wonders, but only for the want of wonder.

23. THE AUTHENTIC HERO 134

Authentic heroism is the will to be oneself.

24. HUMILITY: THE RIGHT ESTIMATE OF
SELF 139

To be humbly aware of one's capacity is to be
most open to opportunities.

25. LET'S COUNT OUR BLESSINGS 144

The cure for worry, pessimism, hopelessness,
despair is to daily count one's blessings.

INDEX 149

1

COMES THE DAWN

The hour that the joyous Aurora
with rosy fingers drives away the
shades of night.[1]   **—RABELAIS**

What's ahead for America? Is there a dawn in the offing? Or is the midnight darkness here to stay, which is to ask, is the disastrous trend of the past few decades to continue? Dictatorship—the total state—our destiny? Liberty but a blessing of the past? These and similar questions are on the lips of freedom devotees. With but few exceptions, they answer themselves forlornly, dejectedly, pessimistically, concluding that there is no hope. No rosy fingers to drive away the shades of night! These are common conclusions, and they are fatal to the aspirations of those who would be free.

Freedom can no more be reborn in hopelessness than wisdom can originate in a robot. For freedom to rise again, there has to be a self-starter and that, at the very minimum,

---

[1] In Roman mythology, Aurora is the goddess of dawn.

1

is a belief in the possibility of freedom. Faith in the possibility of a resurgence of freedom is the starting point, the foundation on which all the intellectual building blocks are laid and erected. Is this a reasonable faith?

As to faith, many philosophers deny that reason has any part to play. For instance, "The Way to see by Faith is to shut the Eye to Reason." However, I go along with the English divine, Sydney Smith: "It is always right that a man should be able to render a reason for the faith that is within him." Are there good reasons for my faith, reasons not seen by many devotees?

I claim no talent as a forecaster. I have no crystal ball and couldn't read it if I had one—nor can anyone else. No one knows what is going to happen in the next minute, let alone in the years ahead. Indeed, no one knows the really significant events that occurred yesterday, the claims of historians to the contrary notwithstanding. However, any assessments we make of the future are *projections of what we observe now*. Witness these words of the distinguished English poet, Lord Tennyson:

> For I dipt into the future, far as
>   human eye could see,
> Saw the Vision of the world and all
>   the wonders that would be;
> Saw the heavens fill with commerce,
>   argosies of magic sails,
> Pilots of the purple twilight, dropping
>   down with costly bales.

Lord Tennyson described a vision of the future based on what he saw happening 130 years ago. And my vision of the future is what I see now, plus what I have seen for the past 43 years. I feel a moral obligation to report my experiences, for I have seen what few others, if any, have witnessed.

What do most of our friends see? *Surface appearances:* the planned economy and the welfare state—socialism— gaining by leaps and bounds. Admittedly, this is horrible to behold, enough to frighten anyone who loves liberty.

In contrast, it has been my privilege to observe what is happening—*beneath the surface* —the wonderful changes in the minds of men and women around the world. For more than four decades, with the freedom philosophy as my major concern, I have lectured and conferred in 22 foreign nations, in several of them numerous times. I have done the same in 48 of our states—several thousand gatherings. In addition, there has been intimate and revealing correspondence over these many years! As a result, I am widely acquainted with devotees of freedom in this and other countries, and *the changes in their thinking.* The reason that bolsters my faith derives from these enlightening experiences.

Perhaps there is no better way to explain what goes on beneath the surface than to relate what went on within me—in 90 minutes! It was during the heyday of the New Deal, a major authoritarian feature of which was the National Industrial Recovery Act—the Blue Eagle, so-called. This scheme of strangling controls was supported by many top businessmen and their organizations: the NAM as well as the National Chamber of Commerce for which I then worked. On hearing that a distinguished businessman in Los Angeles was making critical remarks about the National Chamber policy, I thought it incumbent on me to straighten him out. I went to his office and tried as best I could—for half an hour. Then he proceeded to straighten me out! He talked about the philosophy of freedom for one hour—and won me over to his side. From that moment, the free market, private ownership, limited government way of life has been my major concern.

The explanation of what went on beneath the surface—within me? Know the answer to this and that's all the knowing my thesis requires. It was a happy coincidence: the more or less inadvertent coming together of two levels of learning—of one who knew and of one who wanted to know.

As to my friend and mentor, I have never come upon anyone who saw more clearly through the political fog or sham than he. His explanations were both profound and simple, not only of the fallacies but of the corrective: liberty. And this above all: integrity! This man, Bill Mullendore, was never known to equivocate, to say anything for expediency's sake. Exemplar *par excellence*! This is the plus side of a happy and coincidental get-together.

Now for my side, the minus side. Not knowing much, *and knowing it,* I have always wanted to learn. That's all there is to it. No one can be made to learn. Only those who wish to learn can or ever will do so.

Suppose everyone were a know-nothing or, as the Germans say, a *Dummkopf*. There would be no incentive to learn. But let there arise among us some enlightened souls; then others among us would be stimulated to learn. For it is an observed fact that those out front exert a magnetic force, generating a wanting-to-know-ness.

But how account for those out front? In the absence of anyone to attract them, what fires their pursuit of truth? From whence the magnetism that accounts for their emergence? Emerson phrased the answer to my satisfaction: "We lie in the lap of immense intelligence and we do nothing of ourselves but allow a passage of its beams." Thus, our intellectual, moral, and spiritual leaders are those who have succeeded in allowing "a passage of its beams." The immense intelligence causes them to learn and they, in turn, cause others of us to learn.

Now for my answers to the question, what's going on beneath the surface?

- The quality of thinking is rapidly improving. When we began a program of freedom seminars some twenty years ago, the response often consisted of arguments and confrontations. Today? Eager-beaver, as we say, all participants anxious to learn. Requests for FEE Seminars are now more than we can accommodate.
- Those who, only a short time ago, were students of the freedom philosophy are now teachers. Others are seeking light from them.
- While ours is not a numbers problem—all worthy movements are led by an infinitesimal few—it is encouraging that requests for our literature are on the increase, as is the number of our financial contributors, and on their initiative.
- In the early days of FEE most of our free market, private ownership, limited government presentations were staff-written. Today, excellent manuscripts are coming from ever so many previously unheard of individuals, from this and other countries. Testimony day in and day out: "*The Freeman* gets better each month."
- Thirty years ago there did not exist a consistent literature of the freedom philosophy written in modern

American idiom. Today, the list includes hundreds of volumes ranging all the way from such simple books as Hazlitt's *Economics In One Lesson* to such profound tomes as Mises' *Human Action.*

• Beneath the surface? Bill Mullendores are popping up in many other nations, as well as in growing numbers in the U.S.A. In summary, these are the reasons for my faith.

I am convinced that the joyous Aurora with rosy fingers has already driven away the shades of night. The darkness of midnight has passed and sooner or later will come the dawn.

Admittedly, the momentum of a growing socialism will, for some time, give discouraging surface appearances. But its sustaining force has been replaced—socialism cannot prevail against liberty.

Just one qualification: away with hopelessness, for it is fatal. The evidence beneath the surface is in our favor— hopeful. See it, believe it, and we will win. This is the report that I owe the friends of freedom.

***

Hopefully, the following chapters will lend credence to my optimism or, better yet, to my faith in a rebirth of the good society. And to your faith, if it be lagging a bit.

These chapters contain no original ideas. Rather, each is an attempt more clearly to expose authoritarian fallacies and to better phrase the case for freedom than I have previously accomplished. Briefly, trying to surpass self day in and day out!

One of these days, one of us—perhaps you—will surpass all of us. In any event, let more individuals strive in this manner, and a radiation will result so powerful that others will "tune in"—receive the message. And then? Comes the dawn—for certain!

2

LIFE'S GREATEST OCCUPATION

It is necessary to try to surpass one's self always; this occupation ought to last as long as life.
—QUEEN CHRISTINA

Christina was born to the purple in 1626, and became Queen of Sweden in 1632. A lover of learning, she was tutored by Descartes and other scholars. Christina passed away in 1689, "after a life not lacking in excitement," as one commentator put it. Excitement, indeed, if the above sentence be a sampling of her thinking. What an insight, a revelation that goes to the very root of human destiny—the wellspring of what man is intended to become!

True, to surpass self is the root of human destiny, but too often the roots die aborning. The variety of trivia which pre-empts the time and attention of those who live and have lived is beyond calculation. The vast majority call it quits— life's occupation "achieved"—if they merely keep up with

8

the Joneses. This is an erratic guideline, being no more than self-satisfaction as compared with this person or that! Three samplings:

- *Wealth:* People need sufficient food, clothing, shelter; but what is such a sufficiency? Reflect on the differences in occupations, depending on where and when one lives or lived, and the tendency to stagnate at the generally accepted level. The American Indians of 400 years ago were satisfied with fish, animal skins for clothing, tents, bonfires. To many Americans of our day, it's nothing more than leveling with what they see around them. To millions in our population, it's food stamps or other government handouts. Surpass self? Nary such a thought!
- *Fame:* Everyone enjoys recognition, but even a modicum of praise, applause, notoriety tends to intoxicate ever so many in all walks of life. A fathead is finished, surpassing self not even a dream.
- *Power:* Those whose ambition is to run the lives of others leave no room to run their own. "Power tends to corrupt, and absolute power corrupts absolutely." Corrupt individuals cannot surpass self!

To surpass self, the very *root* of human destiny! The philosopher, William James, made a sage observation:

. . . I am for those tiny, invisible, molecular forces which work from individual to individual, creeping in through the crannies of the world like so many soft *rootlets* . . . but which, if you give them time, will rend the hardest monuments of pride.

To surpass self is the way to do away with pride and, may I suggest, the other frailties as well.

I have believed for several decades that the U.S.A. is in a period of decline and fall, not unlike that of the Roman Empire, and that our salvation is barely thinkable short of an intervention by Divine Providence. On what would such an intervention depend? Would it not be in the form of a few individuals surpassing self, not calling it quits, but moving toward the Overall Enlightenment? Call this, if you will, as did William James, "tiny, invisible molecular forces which work from individual to individual."

It is one thing to assert such a goal but quite another matter to find one's way to it, to avoid the intellectual roadblocks, and remain sensitive to the moral stimuli. What follows are only speculations—explorations as to how one may surpass self, an occupation for life.

To surpass self, humility must rule the soul; otherwise, one claims an insight—a bit of truth—as his own. This is egotism, the opposite of humility, and egotists stagnate rather than grow. Further, injury is done to truth when one proclaims it as his own. The reason is simple: the proclaimer is not the source; innocently or not, he proclaims the wrong source and, thus, the truth is denigrated.

Truth is perceived; it is not originated by any individual. As Emerson wrote:

> We lie in the lap of immense intelligence, which makes us receivers of its truth and organs of its activity. When we discern justice, when we discern truth, we do nothing of ourselves but allow a passage of its beams.

We surpass ourselves only as we succeed in intercepting the beams. And the more accessible to others we make our interceptions—if they in fact be truth—the more will we profit. Fortunately, a truth given to or shared with others is not lost to the giver. As others use the truths we intercept, we gain.

The surpassing of self is a personal *adventure* into the realm of the Unknown. The routes prescribed have ranged all the way from the rantings of gypsies to the wisdom of Augustine's *Confessions*. And the adventurers have ranged from the acclaimed elite to the lowly fishermen of Galilee, from small fry to big shots, from the least of laymen to the holiest of Popes.

This is only to suggest that no infallible route has been staked out for you or me, and for good reason: all who live and have lived are unique—no two remotely alike! Does this mean that we have to go it alone? Of course not! The adventure consists of sorting the wheat from the chaff, the wisdom from the nonsense, and this above all: surpassing each day what we were the day before—headed for the high country of consciousness.

I repeat, to surpass self is an individual achievement. Doubtless, my thinking on this originated many years ago when reading *Across the Unknown* by Stewart Edward White:

[This] development, I had come to realize, is individual. No two men are alike from thumb print to immortal soul. There are no shotgun prescriptions, whether of cult, philosophy or religion. We cannot be helped by rigid regimes. We must have direction, not directions. What is desirable? Which way points our compass? What, in clearer definition, are we after? This is about all we can be told. Recognizable signposts can be planted for us toward the high country, but we alone must find our paths.

So, all I can do is hopefully to serve as a signpost—sharing an experience or two that has been helpful to me—if not in achievement, at least in aspiration.

Here is an example of one route staked out for myself—a means of surpassing—that to most others is unthinkable or undesirable or unworkable or impossible or too time-consuming: *the keeping of a daily Journal.* I made a resolution to do so more than 24 years ago and have not missed a day. Some of the disciplines employed and rewarding to me:

- Making an entry is the first act of each day (the first day of the rest of my life!) and it is initiated with a prayer. It is against the rule to retire unless the day's Journal entry is completed.
- Dictation is also taboo; all entires must be written in longhand or typed. The advantage? Writing demands concentration, and this stimulates the flow of ideas.
- The entries include all that happens: ideas or insights that grace the mind; even who drives me to the airport! My flight experiences are recorded, including conversations with seatmates, if of value. I note comments on my seeming failures and successes as relating to the freedom way of life, inclusions of good thoughts found in my readings; evaluations of all lectures and seminars; on and on—nothing significant omitted. Why the minor entries? Writing puts on paper what's in the mind for the eye to see, thus revealing the need of improvement—of surpassing self day in and day out.

To my way of thinking, Emerson's "we do *nothing* of ourselves but allow a passage of its beams," has a shortcoming with which doubtless he would agree. There is *something* we must do: intercept the beams! These beams, as dreams, are ephemeral—vanishing, evanescent—unless captured. Millions of people have had countless ideas—the intellectual elements of surpassing—about which they are totally unaware. The faithful keeping of a daily Journal is a capturing device. Once your mind knows you mean business, it will cooperate by experiencing the day's events vividly, and retaining them in memory.

When my resolution was made, I had great difficulty, at first, carrying it out. But resolutions are made to be kept, not abandoned willy-nilly. Anyway, in about six months my Journal became a joy. From then on, there has been nothing in the living of each day—life's greatest occupation—that gives me more pleasure; it is unbelievably rewarding!

Not time enough? Perish this careless thought! There is more time to do the worthwhile things in life than any of us knows how to use!

The "beams" of *immense intelligence,* to which Emerson refers, cannot find passage through such obstacles as hopelessness, worry, pessimism, anger, egotism, and the like. The challenge? Remove the obstacles! How? He gives the answer to which I subscribe:

Is not a prayer a study of truth, a sally of the soul into the unfound infinite?—No man ever prayed heartily without learning something.

The prayers to which I allude are not in the form of supplications but, rather, of aspirations. Bear in mind that *immense intelligence* (Something-Beyond-Words) has no appropriate gender, so we resort to He and Thy and the like. Here are several samplings that tend to open one's inner channels:

- *May my living manifest charity, intelligence, justice, love, humility, reverence, and integrity.* To the extent that any of these virtues are absent, to that extent do blockages—ferments of the soul—exist. To "allow a passage of its beams" requires that one's soul be a high-grade conductor of this Radiant Energy. These virtues are the very essence of human conduct—and conductivity.

- *May my daily behaviors be expressions of gratitude for my many, many blessings and opportunities.* An awareness of one's blessings and opportunities is the cure for, the way of warding off, covetousness. Envy is one of the most deadly of sins. No creative energy can pass through a soul so dominated.

- *I pray for Thy blessings upon associates, near and far, past and present, and for the perfection of our ideas and ideals, and our adherence to them.* Other freedom devotees are included because I cannot go it alone; no one can. We learn from each other. My conductivity increases with every gain in enlightenment, whether that initial breakthrough be mine or yours. Thus, to best serve self, my striving for perfection should never be egocentric.

- *May I make progress in removing those faults of mine which stand as obstacles to those of Thy ways which might possibly manifest themselves through me.* I must realize that only an infinitesimal fraction of the *immense intelligence* will be intercepted by me. I have no way of knowing the limits of my capacity but, at the very least, let me not stand in the way.

There are, of course, obstacles galore. There is one, however, which ranks above the others, and the nature of which was perceived by the ancients. Abbreviate the Mosaic Law and it reads something like this:

> God told the people of Israel that if they lived the righteous life they would be graced with abundance, but that there was a snare to this; that is, they might get the idea that the abundance was of their own hands and, if they did, they would suffer hell and damnation.

This applies as rigidly to an abundance of ideas as to a plethora of material goods. For anyone who succeeds in intercepting any rays of the *immense intelligence* to get the notion that he is the source is to dry it up, and thus put an end to any further realization of his potential. To me, intellectual and spiritual sterility is nothing less than hell and damnation!

Reflect on, "I pray for Thy blessings upon associates, past and present." Who, pray tell, are they? They are the ones with whom we associate in ideas and ideals. When and where they were engaged in surpassing themselves matters not at all. What matters is that we draw upon their insights. Ideas intercepted and forgotten sever the association.

Now to the value of keeping a daily Journal. After beginning this chapter, I was skimming through entries made 15 years ago and came upon the following by Edmund Burke written in May 1795:

> How often has public calamity been arrested on the very brink of ruin, by the seasonable energy of a single man? Have we no such man amongst us? I am as sure as I am of my being, that one vigorous mind without office, without situation, without public functions of any kind, (at a time when the want of such a thing is felt, as I am sure it is) I say, one such man, confiding in the aid of God, and full of just reliance in his own fortitude, vigor, enterprise, and

perseverance, would first draw to him some few like himself, and then that multitudes, hardly thought to be in existence, would appear and troop about him.

What a profound observation! It made an impression on me 15 years ago, but then it slipped from my mind. This aspect of my association with that remarkable man ceased to exist. The rereading of my Journal entry renewed the association.

It is not a thoughtless, careless assertion, but a great truth, that once a society has tumbled into an authoritarian mess, as now, there will appear, we know not from where, individuals such as Burke describes. History is replete with examples, ranging from the Perfect Exemplar—Jesus of Nazareth—to Socrates, to Lorenzo the Magnificent, to Adam Smith, to Cobden and Bright, to America's Founding Fathers. Anyone with eyes to see cannot help but observe numerous individuals of this exemplarity among us right now—a time, therefore, not of despair, but of hope.

The formula for salvation is as Christina suggested: *To surpass self—always.* This—life's greatest occupation—is as it should be. Thy blessings on our associates, past and present, near and far!

3

THE HERITAGE WE OWE OUR CHILDREN

*But he who looks into the perfect
law, the law of liberty, and perse-
veres, being no hearer that forgets
but a doer that acts, he shall be
blessed in his doing.*
—JAMES I:25 RSV

A few men who did look into "the law of liberty" bequeathed to present-day Americans a unique heritage. They
were the authors of the Declaration of Independence, the
Constitution, and the Bill of Rights. In what respect were
these political documents unique? First, they unseated
government as the endower of men's rights and placed the
Creator in that role. Second, they more severely limited
government than ever before—for the first time in history,
hardly any organized coercion standing against the release
of creative energy. Result? The greatest outburst of creative
energy ever known, simply because the millions were free to
act creatively as they pleased. Political power diminished
and dispersed beyond the ready grasp of authoritarians who
would run our lives. That was the American miracle!

Each of these founders is thus—according to the Biblical prescription—"blessed in his doing." There are, however, two sides to this law-of-liberty coin. That which has been bequeathed to us carries an obligation that we, if we be doers who act, bequeath this heritage to our children, to oncoming generations! Indeed, it has been written, "It is more blessed to give than to receive."

It is easily demonstrable that giving is the precedent to receiving. The more we give the more we receive. Thus, if we would retain and strengthen that heritage bequeathed to us, we *must* bequeath it to our children. The discharge of this obligation is, in fact, nothing more than *enlightened* self-interest, precisely as is the payment of any debt. When one strives to be a pattern for oncoming generations—our children—he reaches for the best in himself. Help them, help one's self.

Most Americans who give it serious thought would approve acting according to the law of liberty. Yet, in today's world, this is more of a challenge than first meets the eye—more, far more, than was the case with our Founding Fathers. Our politico-economic sires were familiar with the tyranny—authoritarianism—from which they found escape. It was close to their skins, as we say. Their children, however, were a generation removed from the actual experience. We, in our times, are seven generations removed, and have little to go by except a dwindling hearsay. We lack the stimulus to draw a sharp distinction between the Command Society and the Free Society.

There is yet another deterrent to becoming "a doer that acts." By reason of our heritage, a vast majority of this later generation are inclined to take the American miracle as much for granted as the air we breathe—neither of which is much regarded as a blessing.

The "hearer that forgets"—one who lacks awareness of liberty as a blessing—is unlikely to be "blessed in his doing." Nor can such "hearers only" confer on their children the heritage their ancestors bestowed on them. Because of an abysmal unawareness, they receive without gratitude and, for this reason, their failure to give is attended by no sense of wrongdoing. Indeed, unless they act acording to the word, they will continue digging ever deeper into the pocketbooks of their children—a far cry from the law of liberty.

What steps are required, then, for a return to liberty by the millions who have innocently gone along with "leaders" of the Command Society? Assume that our well-meaning individual would do not unto his children that which he would not have had his ancestors do unto him, that he would give to his progeny at least as much as he has received—if not more: where must he begin and where should he go in his thinking? Because it is more blessed to give than to receive, how best can he attend to his own self-interest? These are questions each of us must try to answer, for no one among us is flawless. Improvement in understanding and clarity in exposition is a potentiality of everyone who lives!

It seems obvious that the initial step is to grasp the very essence of Americanism: ". . . that *all* men are endowed by their Creator with certain unalienable Rights, that among these are Life, Liberty. . . ." This acknowledges the Creator as the endower of our rights to life and liberty and, for the first time in the history of nations, casts government out of that role. Until 1776, men had been killing each other by the millions over the age-old question as to which form of authoritarianism should preside as sovereign over human lives and livelihood. The argument, till then, had not been between freedom and authoritarianism, but over what degree of bondage. Our heritage stems from this glorious triumph of human liberty—*everyone* free to act creatively as he chooses. I devoutly believe, along with our Founding Fathers, that the source of human creativity is the Creator.

The next step is to recognize the real meaning of the Constitution and the Bill of Rights. As a student of American history some 65 years ago, I was taught to pay obeisance to these political documents. But even then, it was scarcely more than a gesture, comparable to a salute or a pledge of allegiance to the flag or singing "My Country 'Tis of Thee." Few teachers knew the real meaning in 1776, fewer still when I was a boy, and today? Possibly one in a thousand!

For the true significance, reread the Constitution and the Bill of Rights and note that there are 45 "no's" and "not's" circumscribing governmental power. Reduced to a sentence, they decree: "Government, keep your coercive fingers out of these activities; we reserve these—all of them— to ourselves as free and self-responsible citizens!" The beneficial results were more than I can count but three should be obvious:

1. *Fewer* political know-it-alls meddling in private affairs than ever before!
2. *More* free and self-responsible men and women than ever before!
3. A *greater* outburst of creative energy than ever before!

An agency of society to invoke a common justice and to keep the peace is a social necessity. Its role is to codify the taboos—injustices—and punish any trespass on individual rights. Bear in mind that coercive force is implicit in such an agency. Ideally, it is our protector. *But to expect that coercive force so delegated will be or even can be self-limiting is utterly absurd.* Yet that is the common view today. This carelessness is fatal to a good society. Why? Our hoped-for protector turned plunderer, as we are witnessing.[1]

There is one remedy, and one only: Eternal vigilance on the part of the citizenry is the price of liberty. How be vigilant? Master the "no's" and "not's" set forth in the Constitution and the Bill of Rights and insist with all the reason one can muster that the taboos limiting runaway power be strictly observed. If we would bequeath to our children that which our Founding Fathers bequeathed to us, this is the price. Is that price too high? Not if we can discover where our self-interest lies!

Given these foundations for enlightened self-interest, one may appreciate, with Henry Hazlitt, that economics "is the science of tracing the effects of some proposed or existing policy not only on some special interest in the short run, *but on the general interest in the long run.*" Our children's interest, as well as our own!

A sampling of how one, thus enlightened, will react to some of the modern proposals for political intervention:

---

[1]There's a delightful story of how Congressman Davy Crockett stumbled into a keen awareness of the distinction between protection and plunder. Complimentary copy of "Not Yours to Give" available on request from FEE.

- He hears: The way to prosperity is to increase farm prices. He reacts: This makes food dearer to city workers.
- He hears: The way to national wealth is by means of governmental subsidies. He reacts: This is to claim that more goods result from increased taxes.
- He hears: The road to recovery is to increase wage rates. He reacts: This is to say that recovery depends on higher costs of production! On and on, ad infinitum![2]

A good guideline by John Stuart Mill: "Whatever crushes individuality is despotism, by whatever name it may be called." Our Founding Fathers saw eye to eye on despotism and declared their independence of it. May we follow in their footsteps! And more good counsel: "Don't hoard good ideas. The more you radiate [share], the more you germinate." This is another way of asserting that "It is more blessed to give than to receive."

The heritage we owe our children is to look into the perfect law of liberty, be a doer of the word and, thus, blessed in our doing.

---

[2]These examples paraphrase ideas from *Economics In One Lesson* by Henry Hazlitt, available from FEE.

4

OUR PROBLEMS: BLESSINGS IN DISGUISE

Don't think of problems as difficulties, think of them as opportunities for action. Hard as they are, they may turn out to be blessings in disguise.

—C. F. KLEINKNECHT

Is it not true that most people look upon their problems only as difficulties? Even worse, they regard their problems as dreaded invasions of the serene life. Why this perverse view? Problems should be likened to birth pains; the good life has its genesis in them and their "painful" overcoming. Let's see if we can make the case for *joyfully* overcoming them.

This thesis, obviously, is premised on the good life, and that needs definition. Simply stated, the good life is the opposite of stagnation or retirement; it is incompatible with the listless life. It is, instead, emergence, evolution, hatching—day by day growing along the lines of one's creative uniqueness. There is no destination or point of arrival in the good life but, rather, a perpetual *becoming*.

Wrote Saint Augustine, "Happiness consists in the attainment of our desires, and in our having *only the right*

23

desires." If the purpose of life be an expanding awareness, perception, consciousness, what desire could be higher than expanding one's consciousness into a harmony with Infinite Consciousness? Pascal put it this way: "Happiness is neither within us only, nor without us; it is the union of ourselves with God." Of all forms of happiness this one must, in my judgment, be assessed as joyous!

The basic problem that confronts the three billion people who inhabit this earth relates to survival—to having any life at all. The first need is for food, the second for fiber. Solve these basic demands or perish!

Parenthetically, it is enlightening to recognize what it is that largely accounts for the shortness of life of a majority of the billions who are graced with birth. In a sense, it is a lack of "business" knowledge—knowledge of what is our business and what is none of our business. In India, to cite but one example, people perish by the millions because dictocrats—the know-it-alls—engage in what is none of their business. If we are more blessed with longevity in the U.S.A., it is because here, more than elsewhere, each tends to what is his own business. Hardly any freedom of choice in India, a great deal of it in the U.S.A.

For many people in some lands, life has no more problems once their needs are met for food and fiber. And equally satisfied are most Americans who live in relative luxury. Problems, regarded as painful nuisances, are in the past tense—glory be! This wrong attitude is widespread.

It is his attitude toward problems that makes or breaks the individual. "Problems make or kill you," wrote the remarkable Austrian economist, Böhm-Bawerk. According to one of his students, Ludwig von Mises, they killed his teacher.

Böhm-Bawerk, who had a profound understanding of what ought to be, saw the world going to pot as a result of Marxism. The problem pained him; the resulting distress shortened his life, as distress usually does.

Analogous to my theme is the story of a Persian farmer named Hafed. He left his farm and searched for a diamond mine, finding none. Years later, long after the weary and penniless Hafed had died tragically in a strange land, another Persian while digging in Hafed's deserted garden discovered the diamond mines of Golconda, the richest ever uncovered in the ancient world.[1]

The point is that those problems we tend to deplore may very well be diamonds—hidden in one's own mind, not elsewhere.

Epictetus, the Roman slave who rose to become one of the world's great philosophers, declared that "It is difficulties [problems] which show what men are."

It is reported that Thomas Edison made 50,000 experiments before he succeeded in producing the storage battery. He was asked if he didn't get discouraged working so long without results. "Results!" he exclaimed, "Why I learned 50,000 things I didn't know before." His 50,000 problems were that many blessings in disguise.

What, then, is the formula? First, solve the problem of obtaining food and fiber; this makes survival possible. Second, find a way to overcome the Command Society and achieve freedom of choice; this makes plenitude possible for one and all. But keep right on finding problems to solve! This is only the beginning.

---

[1] See Prologue to *The Key to Peace* by Clarence Manion (Bensenville, Illinois: The Heritage Foundation, Inc., 1975).

Having achieved the aforementioned things of this world—accomplishments of this mortal moment—look next to the immortal: life eternal. What aspect of man has the potential to be everlasting? Is it not his *consciousness*—the mind's intellectual development of thought—spirit, if you prefer? In my view, it is this and this alone which is immortalized, that lives forever. It qualifies as the highest of "right desires," for it has to do with the expanding of one's own consciousness, as nearly as possible, into a harmony with Infinite Consciousness.

The goal is nothing less than ascension in consciousness, and this is a step by step procedure. As one problem is solved or overcome, look for a higher one. For it is an observed fact that the art of becoming is composed of acts of overcoming. Although each problem will at first appear difficult and doubtless painful, once overcome it will be assessed as joyful—a blessing in disguise.

Bear in mind that problems in this higher realm are not thrust upon us as are earthly obstacles, such as the Command Society. To the contrary, they must be searched for and then overcome. Explore the unknown for problems as a means to an expanding consciousness—for gracing morality with immortality.

Finally, it becomes more and more self-evident that the free society will replace the Command Society to the extent that morality is immortalized. Why this assertion? Ours is a moral problem! It follows then that we should labor in the higher realm to free ourselves in the earthly realm. Then, indeed, will our problems—all of them—be blessings in disguise.

5

THE ROLE OF DIFFERENCES

We can never be sure that the opinion we are endeavoring to stifle is false opinion; and even if we were sure, stifling would be an evil still. **—JOHN STUART MILL**

The following reflections are inspired by two incidents: (1) a statement in today's paper by a famous "conservative" politician standing foursquare for our socialized postal system, and (2) a letter from an ailing and scholarly gentleman who prides himself on being a freedom devotee: "Thank goodness for medicare."

Shakespeare wrote: "How use doth breed a habit in a man." Habit has me cringing at these typical examples of giving away the case for freedom. But reason suggests that my habit is more to be censured than these differences! The counsel of reason?

- Were everyone identical in thinking and doing, all would perish. Our differences—individual variations— lie at the root of human welfare.
- Truth flowers from the discovery of error. Find what's

27

wrong and the mind opens to what's right—exploration ensues.

- Criticizing the person who advocates what I believe to be wrong *blinds* him to what I believe to be right. Rather than being drawn to my view, he is repelled by such a tactic; it sparks his defense mechanism and closes his mind—at least to me. Stifling *is* an evil!

Let anyone freely speak his views, even if they be those of Karl Marx! Discovering the error in such views opens the mind to the truths of human liberty. Springboards! This is by way of proudly confessing that I am irrevocably committed to the proposition that some opinions are false; for instance, those favoring authoritarianism in its numerous forms. On this, I side with the English poet, William Cowper:

> Tis liberty alone that gives the flower
> Of fleeting life its lustre and perfume,
> *And we are weeds without it. All constraint*
> *Except what wisdom lays on evil men*
> *Is evil.*

Briefly, all constraint against the freedom of any individual to act creatively as he chooses is evil; it is as false as striving for hell and damnation! I, for one, am settled on this view, now and hereafter.

However, it is not my intention here to dwell on the differences between the dictocrats and freedom devotees.[1] Rather, it is to comment on the differences that crop up on the freedom side of the fence and to reflect on their value. My theme is that these differences play a teaching role in the learning process of each of us.

[1]This I have done in the chapter, "The Blessings of Diversity" in *Castles in the Air* (FEE, 1975), pp. 73-77.

How many in the U.S.A. today really believe in the freedom way of life? How many oppose the Command Society, which for several decades has been so rapidly on the upswing? Who can tell? Certainly, the 50,000 requesting and receiving our studies is no measure: these few are no more than a mere fraction of those who believe in freedom. The vast majority has never heard of our efforts devoted exclusively to private ownership, free market, limited government ideas and ideals. Doubtless, most of them never will, nor is it necessary that they do!

To be a believer is one thing. What to do about it is quite another matter. It is in the realm of what-to-do—methodology, not ideology—that there are glaring differences among freedom devotees. Why are these differences blessings in disguise? One reason: Who among us can be *absolutely* certain that his methodology is correct? Not I, for sure—a compelling reason why I must do my best to keep an open mind as to method!

To be consistent, anyone who says, "Hurrah for our differences"—as I do—should not argue that the differences be resolved, that others adopt my method or yours. Not at all! Let the differences run rampant. Seek neither agreement nor praise, only what's right. For, who knows, someone's *glaring* differences may turn out to be the key to correct and effective method. If we keep our minds open, each explaining his own ideas as best he can, we may eventually learn what the right way is. In all humility, I believe there is a right way.

For 43 years the freedom philosophy has been my major concern. I have been exposed, as much as anyone, to countless techniques for its advancement. Many of these I have tried and many I have abandoned as *seemingly* futile or downright harmful. However, I do not ask that my judgment prevail, for what *seems* true and the only right way to me may not be the best and last word. What then is my role? It is precisely the same as yours: openly honest and frank in presenting what seems to be right, and open-minded as to what in fact *may* be right and wrong. Catholicity! Sample a few of my differences with others, taking note of the fact that I am trying to learn from each difference.

Here is a proposal from a freedom devotee: *A convention to be held at FEE, the participants to write a new Constitution.*

Of all places not to hold such a convention would be in the halls of an institution so at odds philosophically with majority opinion. Our 50,000 friends would hear about and doubtless read the document; but if it were widely publicized, it would be popularly ridiculed. But that's only the beginning of my difference. What did I learn from this? That never in American history should a new Constitution be more ardently opposed than now. Why? It would be but a reflection or echoing of the preponderant leadership thinking of our time. As a consequence, it would resemble the Communist Manifesto![2]

Concentrate at the political level; set the politicians straight!

What do I learn from this commonly recommended tactic?

---

[2] If this claim appears as farfetched, have a careful look at the ten points of the Communist Manifesto and observe how much of it we have already adopted in the U.S.A.

I beg to differ, because this approach presumes that its practitioners have mastered the freedom philosophy. The fact? Not a one of us has more than scratched the surface. All of us are neophytes! This is an acknowledgment necessary for an improved understanding, be it yours or mine.

I repeat, whatever shows forth on today's political horizon reflects our preponderant leadership thinking. The Declaration, the Constitution and the Bill of Rights were a reflection of the leadership thinking two centuries ago. Not perfect, but history's best—by far! Note that these documents are no more than scraps of paper today, because our leadership thinking is too corrupt to sustain such wisdom.

Let our thinking improve until those in public office no longer vie with each other as to the good they can do for us with our money. Improve our thinking and methods, and they will contend with each other to advance free market, private ownership, limited government ideas and ideals. Thinking, good or bad, is cause; politics, good or bad, is effect. Doesn't it make sense to concentrate at the cause level rather than to "spin our wheels" at the effect level?

The mess we observe today is but the effect of hanging onto yesterday's poor thinking. What's past is past, the effects no less than the causes. Wrote the Bard of Avon, "Things without remedy, should be without regard; what is done is done." The lesson? Concentrate on the improvement of one's thinking and understanding, for out of it may come a return to freedom—the blessings of liberty! That's what this difference has to teach me.

Sell the masses, the man in the street!
Here again is the presupposition that the would-be seller

has mastered his subject. For a good example of the man in the street, let these "salesmen" look in the mirror.

We frown on those politicians who are so egotistical that they believe they can run our lives better than we can. But what of those who claim to know precisely what it is the rest of us must learn?

Learning is an individualistic, taking-from, not an injection-into, process. Learning is our task, not selling. If I have some knowledge of our philosophy, which is my responsibility, and if another wants to know about it, which is his responsibility, my counsel will be sought. It is only when one seeks understanding that he absorbs it into his tissues. Indeed, there is an accurate measuring rod as to how well one has progressed himself: observe how many are seeking one's tutorship. If none, there is homework to be done.

We hear countless enthusiasts whose proclaimed mission is to "reach" this or that group or class of people, such as teachers, students, clergy, employees, on and on. My difference with this tactic? Instead of trying to reach for anyone, let's see if we can gain enough competency so that others will reach for us. Seeking and reaching are one and the same—the only path to learning. This is the way it should be. Suppose I could insinuate my ideas into the minds of others. Then they might do the same to me— making me the victim of every inanity and insanity on earth! Thank you, no!

Make the teaching of free enterprise compulsory in the public schools.

Several states have already voted such a law and more are

in the offing. What a quack remedy—an utter absurdity!
Assume yourself to be a student and, at the same time, a
freedom devotee, and that the teaching of socialism were
made compulsory. Nothing but resentment! You would, if
permitted, drop out of school. "Free enterprise teaching,"
when compulsory, is no less revolting. I can think of no
method more at odds with our philosophy than the *compulsory teaching of freedom!* What a contradiction in terms!

Further, how many teachers in the public schools today
have the slightest idea of the free market, private ownership, limited government way of life? With rare exceptions, they are unaware of the proper textbooks and have
never even heard of Ludwig von Mises and others of his
kind. I accepted an invitation to discuss our philosophy with
27 teachers who are now *compelled* to "teach free enterprise." Of that group, there was only one with an awareness
of what I was talking about. The bright spot in that lonesome
experience was his understanding.[3]

We must form one, big, strong organization!

This tactic has been suggested over and over again for the
past 30 years. Instead of FEE and a thousand and one other
"outfits" working along their respective and diverse
lines—each embracing what it believes the right method—
amalgamate, get together, merge into a powerful ONE!
Away with all of these differences!

The various organizations working on behalf of freedom
differ from one another in several respects, but the major
difference has to do with method or tactics. Those who

---

[3]For a detailed explanation of my differences, see "Looking in the
Mirror," a chapter in *To Free or Freeze* (FEE, 1972), pp. 48-55.

plead for one big organization are confessing an inability to distinguish one method from another, when deciding which organization to support. In effect, "I can't give to all of them nor can I tell one from the other so, for my sake, relieve me of having to tell the difference."

This attempt at amalgamation, if accepted, would bring to an end all honest convictions—differences—as to correct and effective method. Instead? One great big methodological potpourri! I, for one, prefer open competition. I still insist, "hurrah for our differences!" Why? Just as every socialistic cliche serves as a steppingstone toward making a better case for freedom, so does every tactical error committed by freedom devotees inspire a refinement of correct method.

Finally, the refinement of my belief that ours is exclusively a learning and not a selling problem, poses a rare and more significant question: What lies beyond knowing how to explain the fallacies of socialism and to espouse instead the principles of freedom? More—ever so much more!

Liberty—"we are weeds without it"—will not grace a people who are slumping into apathy, who quit thinking for selves, or who let prosperity—a by-product of liberty—go to their heads. Merely scrutinize what's going on. Liberty and "the permissive society" cannot be companion experiences.

What then must we learn? To perceive and to adhere to the virtues—integrity, statesmanship, moral exemplarity—on a higher plane than has ever been known. Each advancing age must be so featured, for this is implicit in the evolution of humanity. Short of this, the historical sequence of evolution/devolution, evolution/devolution will go its wearisome way, awaiting the day when men will accept more responsibility for their own destiny than now.

Should we do—right now—what the Cosmic Scheme obviously calls for, historians of the future will write of our era, "The Great and Unprecedented Moral Renaissance." How better can you or I employ our lives and potential talents than to participate in this reawakening to the principles and practices of those virtues that are the very foundations of freedom!

And I come back now to my opening theme that chief among those virtues is tolerance of honest differences as to the methods of achieving and practicing freedom. We are agreed that freedom is our goal, so let us extend to every man the respect due him, and carefully study his methods in order to improve our own.

6

TWO DIRECTIONS AT ONCE

*He that wrestles with us strength-
ens our nerves and sharpens our
skill. Our antagonist is our helper.*
—EDMUND BURKE

More than 20 years ago Henry Hazlitt remarked to me that
the country is going in two directions at once! His explanation prompted me to write on the subject in the October 1956
Freeman.

It is time to re-examine that thesis. These two decades
reveal a profound truth: Success is not a destination but a
journey! Briefly, we never arrive at an ideal situation; at
best, we make progress toward what is true and righteous.
And we need assurance now and then that we are in fact
making progress.

So far as the millions are concerned, socialism is more
agreeably accepted today than a year ago or two decades
ago. It may continue to grow. On the other hand. there is a
small but growing minority of persons who are becoming
more skilled, articulate, and ardent devotees of socialism's
opposite: the free market, private ownership, limited gov-

ernment way of life with its moral and spiritual antecedents.

Detailed confirmation of this phenomenon is not the object of this essay. Henry Hazlitt is as keen as any observer of ideological and politico-economic trends. Further, we at FEE may draw upon 30 years of specializing in this area, our considerable correspondence, and our discussions with individuals and groups from varied walks of life and around the nation. It is clear to us that while millions are accepting socialism, there are thousands who are becoming skilled in understanding and explaining the freedom philosophy.

My sole object here is to suggest to persons who perceive the meaning of liberty that the mass movement does not warrant despair! The movement toward socialism is the condition which is motivating our own search for what is true and righteous.

First, a bit of background: The Constitution and Bill of Rights confirmed and aimed to perpetuate a novel theory of a servant government of strictly limited powers. In the decades that followed, citizens did not turn to government for succor, for goverment was so limited that it had nothing on hand to dispense, nor did it then have the power to take from some and give to others. In the absence of any political nursemaid, there developed a remarkable self-reliance among the people. Further, government was limited to defending life and the honest fruits of men's labors; it was not empowered to inhibit the creative actions of citizens. As a consequence, there was a freeing of creative human energy. In short, here was political liberty, the like of which had never existed elsewhere. Self-reliant men and women, freed from predators and freed from restraints on their creativity, brought into existence what is loosely referred to as "the American heritage."

Americans, however, began to take the blessings of liberty for granted. Unprecedented well-being came to be regarded as an act of nature; progress seemed as inevitable as the sun's appearance in the morning. That the practice of difficult human virtues and political wisdom lay at the root of this new-world miracle was forgotten or, more likely, never learned by new generations. Americans, for the most part, were unaware of the rationale on which their magnificent edifice was erected. The intellectual and moral foundation weakened and the limitations on government were relaxed. Disaster—in the form of a return to the old-world pattern of sovereign state and servant people—was only a matter of time.

Societal arrangements, be they good or bad, have a tempo, a rapidity of change, far slower than that of human beings. Thus, most citizens, enjoying the forward thrust that was possible under limited governmental structures, came to believe that the ever-increasing governmental intervention they subsequently voted was responsible for their prosperity and well-being. Today, they fail to see that the genuine bounties in their situation are but the result of an earlier momentum precisely as they fail to recognize the bogus aspects of present "prosperity." Self-reliance and freed energies have made for such wealth that they can, for a time at least, take government pap without apparent immediate injury. And many believe the pap to be the cause of their vitality.

The above broad conclusions are cited only as preface to this brief thesis. The crack in American constitutional theory certainly was not observed when it first occurred. I must admit that I had no realization as to what had happened—what was happening—until 1932. Only a few persons seemed aware of what was taking place by the late twenties. I recall my amazement in reading, much later, a little book published in 1923 in which the author, John W. Burgess, saw clearly what had already happened at that early date! Yet, it is unlikely that even Dr. Burgess saw very much prior to 1923 or he would have written his book earlier. In his *Recent Changes In American Constitutional Theory,* he traced the beginning of the breakdown to 1898.[1] Subsequent events led first to one thing and then another, culminating in the adoption of the Sixteenth Amendment in 1913. With the adoption of the progressive income tax, we officially disclaimed the theoretical correctness of limited government, private property, and the free market.

But find those rare few who saw the meaning of these cracks in our structure at the time they happened! The adage that "things have to get worse before they can get better" contains an element of truth. Figuratively, only a lonely soul or two cried out against this sin in 1913. Why? It was then no more than an affront to good theory. This wholly unAmerican device had to grow up, have a pocketbook sting in its operation, gain millions of adherents, before any significant opposition could form. Today, with this theoretical devil the monster it was born to be, there are numerous citizens who would vote for repeal if given a chance. But it has taken the monster stage to generate the significant opposition! The

---

[1] Dr. John W. Burgess was the founder and for many years the head of the Department of Political Science and Constitutional Law, Columbia University.

mere infraction of good theory may disturb a few good theoreticians. But those early infractions do not excite or awake the populace.

We accepted a communistic doctrine when we adopted the Sixteenth Amendment—"from each according to ability, to each according to need"—so it was natural that socialism in all its forms would follow in due course. One could hardly expect a people to embrace this plank from the *Communist Manifesto* and at the same time have any strong misgivings about other socialistic theories and practices.

The record speaks for itself; we have been and are still going down the socialistic route! Our national policy is consistent with the Sixteenth Amendment. But, and this is the important point, this very trend is generating an opposite ideological movement. Further, the socialistic direction appears to be a preliminary state of affairs necessary to hatch its opposition. Let me attempt an explanation of what at first glance appears to be an anomaly.

Since error (socialism or whatever) opposes truth, one might suppose that error has no function. Yet error does have a role to play—as a steppingstone to truth! Man emerges, evolves, goes in the direction of truth, by an *overcoming* process. Overcoming presupposes something to overcome. To take even a simple step presupposes something stepped on. Ascendancy presupposes lower positions. A movement Godward presupposes ungodliness to shun.

Consider these opposites: evil and virtue, error and truth. Do we not witness mighty opposites similarly at work on every hand? For instance, would we have any notion of "up" were not a gravitational force pulling us down? Would "light" be in our vocabulary if there were no darkness?

Would we have the concept of justice were there no injustice? Isn't hate the evil trait that permits us to see love as a virtue? Where does the passion for security arise except from fear of insecurity? And isn't all intelligence a degree of understanding and wisdom relative to ignorance?

Inquiring further into nature's mysteries, and going as far as science has probed into the ultimate constitution of things, we learn that "every substance is a system of molecules in motion and every molecule is a system of oscillating atoms and every atom is a system of *positive* and *negative* electricity." Or, to quote the late physicist, Robert A. Millikan, "All elastic forces are due to the *attraction* and *repulsions* of electrons." Polarity at the very root of things!

It would appear that the mainspring of all creations, of all variation, of all progress, comes by reason of this tension of the opposites, sometimes called the law of polarity. If there were no tension, nothing to overcome, there would be no "becoming," no movement toward higher orders. Obstacles, I contend, have their role. They—error and evil—are deficiencies to step on, to rise above. Without them, we are incapable of perceiving any *above*.

There is abundant evidence that this tension of the opposites has been long and well understood by a few. Several selections:

> Then welcome each rebuff
> That turns earth's smoothness rough,
> Each sting that bids not sit nor
>   stand but go!
> Be our joy three-parts pain!
> Strive, and hold cheap the strain;

Learn; nor account the pang;
   dare, never grudge the throe!
          —Robert Browning

Adversity is the first path to truth.
             —Byron

Bad times have a scientific value.
These are occasions a good learner
would not miss.

           —Emerson

Are Afflictions aught but Blessings
in disguise?

         —David Mallet

Let us be patient! These severe
   afflictions
Not from the ground arise
But oftentimes celestial
   benedictions
Assume this dark disguise.
            —Longfellow

O benefit of ill! now I find true
That better is by evil still made
   better.

         —Shakespeare

Truth, crushed to earth, shall rise
   again;
Th' eternal years of God are
   hers;
But Error, wounded, writhes in
   pain,
And dies among his worshipers.
            —Bryant

The road to valor is builded by
adversity.
                                    —Ovid

Error is the discipline through
which we advance.
                    —William Ellery Channing

Dark error's other hidden side is
truth.
                                    —Victor Hugo

Shall error in the round of time
Still father Truth?
                                    —Tennyson

The foregoing are thoughts which suggest that a growing socialism performs a positive function.

A few additional thoughts as to what the socialistic system is: It is the opposite of the free market or willing exchange economy. It is forced, unwilling, coerced exchange. It rests on the suppression of creative human energy. It is the substitution of authoritarianism for market phenomena.

To commandeer, that's it! Webster defines "commandeer:" "to take arbitrary possession of; to commandeer men or goods." Illustrations: The honest fruits of our labors are commandeered to make up the deficits of government intervention into the light and power field, as in TVA; into the construction industry, as in government housing; into health, as in medicare. No one can possibly name all the commandeering by our thousands of goverments. However, this we can deduce: One's earnings or capital would be employed otherwise if free choice rather than commandeering prevailed. Keep in mind that the very essence of ownership is control; that which I do not control, I do not own! The political order that features commandeering can be appropriately termed, "The Command Society."

Freedom loses ground because of our taking-for-granted attitudes, our lethargy, our unawareness. But liberty, the ability to act creatively as we please, is a prerequisite to evolution, emergence. Eventually, we must be free; it is ordained in the Cosmic Order. And we will be free! True, our freedom is conditioned on our understanding of its nature and purpose. Merely observe what's taking place.

The growing socialism is creating its own anti-agents. Abhorrence of it is stimulating many Americans of all ages to study and reflect on the nature of freedom. Contemplating freedom, they are discerning its deeper values and, as a result, are regaining their faith in free men. They are coming to understand and, in understanding, are learning to explain. They are seeing that the purpose of wealth, a by-product of freedom, is not for a recess from life's activities but, instead, is to release them to work harder than ever at those creative ventures peculiar to their own uniqueness. They are seeing that freedom is the gateway to new levels of the intellect and of the spirit.

Socialism is freedom's opposite, the error, the primitive order to be stepped on and overcome; it is the tension that can spring man into a more wholesome concept of life's high purpose. And this is the role of socialistic error in man's *becoming!*

Be not distraught that we are no more than an infinitesimal minority. For, as Burke observed, our antagonist is indeed our helper. Be jubilant and have faith!

7

PRE-EMPTORS: AGENTS OF DESTRUCTION

*You can only make men free when
they are inwardly bound by their
own sense of responsibility.*
—WILLIAM ERNEST HOCKING

I am indebted to Verna Hall for a profound bit of wisdom:

To the extent that an individual turns the responsibility
for self over to another or allows government to take it
away, *to that extent is the very essence of one's being
removed.*

With this insight, let us reflect on the radically contrasted
types of society in which men have found themselves. The
most common type, by far, is the Command Society,
bearing many names: Serfdom, Feudalism, Mercantilism,
Socialism, Nazism, Fascism, Communism, the Planned
Economy, the Welfare State. This type is featured by
commanders ranging from kings and commissars to
present-day politicians and bureaucrats—all engaged in
running people's lives. The Command Society has never
been totally imposed, but only approximated; if fully im-
plemented, everyone would perish! Even in Russia and
China there has been and still is an enormous leakage of
creative human energy.

The alternative is the Free Society, with each individual in charge of his own life. This is an ideal, in a sense—never fully achieved—most nearly approximated for a time in England and even more so in the U.S.A.

So-called "citizens" of the Command Society are responsible to political overlords. Self-realization is the exception and not the rule. The highest expectations for the vast majority are crumbs from the ruler's table. Can this be all there is to man's earthly purpose?

The essential feature of a Free Society is responsibility for self. I am responsible, not for you or anyone else, but solely for my own growth in awareness, perception, consciousness. My responsibility is thus to truth, righteousness, Infinite Consciousness. Responsibility for self is the very essence of individuality. It is the intellectual, moral, and spiritual rock that serves as the foundation for human emergence. As Hocking wrote, men are only "free when they are inwardly bound by their own sense of responsibility."

This thesis requires answers to at least three questions:

1. Why are pre-emptors agents of destruction?
2. Who, aside from political dictocrats, are pre-emptors?
3. What might the remedies be?

Take note of this fact: Any time any activity is pre-empted, all thought as to how it would be conducted by free and self-responsible people is deadened. For instance, when governments take command of welfare problems—pre-empts them—citizens tend to lose personal concern for those in distress. "That's the government's problem!" This is how political and bureaucratic authors of state welfarism become agents of destruction. What have they destroyed? Nearly all thought as to how citizens would behave in the absence of such political intervention. How might you and I otherwise tend to act? We would share our last loaf of bread with a neighbor in distress. The practice of Judeo-Christian charity would be extravagant beyond all present expectations. Why, then, is private charity so little in evidence today? Because governments have pre-empted that function.

For another example that more clearly makes the point, consider mail delivery.

Our postal system is a socialistic institution—a mechanism of the Command Society. Its record? As all users know, a dramatic increase in rates, enormous deficits mounting annually, and service deteriorating rather than improving.

Observe the effect of this pre-emption: no intelligent thought of what this type of communication would be like among a free and self-responsible people. And for more reasons, far more, than first meets the eye. Conceded, there are many among us who urge the total abandonment of this Command Society mechanism but without the slightest idea of what the freedom alternative would be. Why this blindness as to the results of freedom? The answer is: the actions of free men are quite impossible to foresee!

It is one thing to believe that competition affords more efficient service than does a monopoly. Indeed, this very belief is implicit in the arguments of government officials who refuse to permit private delivery of mail: the U.S. Postal Service couldn't stand the competition; someone else would do it more efficiently and at less cost to the customer.

But as long as the monopoly is coercively maintained, there is no legal way to prove that the cost of performing an identical service would be lower under competition—or how much lower. Nor can it be proved beyond doubt that competitive private enterprise would indeed perform precisely the same services now available through the Postal monopoly.

But this is the whole point of anyone who believes in the blessings of competition as the most efficient way to provide the goods and services customers are willing and able to pay for. Such faith must concede that no one knows or can know in advance just the form in which the postal service would emerge and develop were everyone free to devote his own ingenuity and time and scarce resources toward serving the ever-changing demands of willing customers in a free market.

If all those changing conditions could be foreseen by any one individual, there is no logical reason why he could not make socialism work. But that is the whole case against socialism and for competitive private enterprise: the unknown is not foreseeable or predictable with certainty; conditions change, and freedom affords us the best possible chance to cope with those changes. If one believes the Postal monopoly should be abolished, it is in part because he has witnessed miraculous market developments in the delivery of items other than mail.

Take voice delivery. How far could the human voice be delivered prior to the beginning of the Bell system a century ago? Perhaps 50 yards! In the meantime—*the miracle of the market*—around the earth, not at the speed of sound but at the speed of light, that is, in the same fraction of a second you could hear my voice half the span of a football field. Those who find this not particularly amazing are nonetheless reluctant to entrust the delivery of mail to the unhampered and unpredictable ingenuity of a free and self-responsible people!

Suppose Leonardo da Vinci, who believed that men might some day fly like birds, had been clairvoyant enough to see five centuries into the future. We can imagine his amazement at today's planes and their performance. Yet we lack the imagination to visualize the future of mail delivery, and so we lack the courage and faith to trust the job to the miraculous market.

Why this fear to try—this lack of faith in the potential wonders that might be ours? There are at least two reasons: (1) we cannot foresee the unknown and, thus, we are not attracted to the unimaginable, and (2) the moment a miracle is wrought, we take it as much for granted as the air we breathe. Who stands today in wonder and respect at getting a friend on the phone in Hong Kong as quickly as one can call a next-door neighbor? The miracle is old hat! We no longer give it a second thought—unless the phone goes dead.

To me, the Command Society is a carry-over of barbarism, whereas the Free Society is the flowering of civilization. Why, then, so much more widespread approval of the former than the latter? The reason, as I now see it, is this: *The way the free market works its wonders is a phenomenon so far advanced in human evolution that it borders on the celestial!* Some of us understand that it does work these wonders but do not understand how to clearly explain this process which ranks so high in the spiritual realm.

Years ago, I observed that no person knows how to make such a "simple" thing as an ordinary wooden lead pencil.[1] Yet, that year, we made 1,600,000,000 pencils in the U.S.A. Were we to grasp this single miracle of the free market, we would know that there is not a person who knows how to operate a postal service or how to deliver the human voice at the speed of light. No one knows for sure what electricity is! Make a jet plane? It is to laugh! The only reason why a Command Society can deliver mail at all is because there is a leakage of creative human energy.

Why the claim that this phenomenon is so high in the spiritual realm? Ludwig von Mises gives us the answer:

Production [a pencil, mail delivery, a jet plane] is a spiritual, intellectual, and ideological phenomenon. . . . What distinguishes our conditions [the Free Society] from those of our ancestors who lived one thousand or twenty thousand years ago [the Command Society] is not something material but something spiritual. *The material changes are the outcome of spiritual changes.*[2]

Everything by which we live and thrive—the material— has its origin in the spiritual, in the sense that an idea is spiritual, or an invention, discovery, insight, intuitive flash.

Why, then, does the Free Society work its wonders? Why, when no one knows how to make a pencil, do we have such a proliferation of goods and services? *The spiritual forces—tiny ideas by everyone—are free to flow!* Result of this free flow? Ideas configurate and show forth in everything from billions of pencils to jet planes. This explains why

---

[1] "I, Pencil," copy of reprint on request from FEE.

[2] See *Human Action* (Chicago: Henry Regnery Company. Third Revised Edition, 1966), p. 142.

the wisdom of the free market is infinitely greater than that which exists in a Socrates or Edison or any one person.

Now the question: Why are the dictocrats—the pre-emptors—agents of destruction? What do they destroy? *The spiritual—the very essence of one's being!* There may be a few exceptions but most people fail to generate ideas on activities that have been pre-empted.

Aside from members of our present Command Society, who are these pre-emptors? All persons who turn to the dictocrats seeking their own gain at the expense of others. And it matters not whether the "gains" sought are food stamps, or tariffs, or higher than market wages, or a Gateway Arch, or whatever. By such actions, they ally themselves with the Command Society.

It should be noted with regard to all governmental welfare programs that function by the formula, "from each according to ability, to each according to need," that these "needy" allies of the Command Society have no limit. They feed and multiply upon the subsidies until they become wholly useless to themselves or to anyone else—except as voters bribed to keep their political benefactors in power. This is the tremendous political appeal of socialism—parasitism pursued to the death of the last host, and last hope.

Finally, what might the remedies be? How are the pre-emptors to be unseated? Should we expect Command Society personnel to take the initiative in ridding themselves of coercive powers? Indeed not, for they have substituted self-exaltation for self-realization and, thus, are addicted to their dictatorial role. Lording it over us for our benefit, or so they naively believe.

And expect no initiative from their pre-empting allies. The "guaranteed life" is for them an attractive way of life or they would not have sought it in the first place.

Where look for the remedy? To the few who have gained an awareness of how the free market works its wonders. Purists? Maybe, at least in their singleness of purpose and the wholeness of their understanding. But hardly so in their manner of living, for they too must live in the world as it is. And that world often compels them to engage in ways of life that strain their concepts of righteousness. To name but a single item, I use the postal service of the Command Society. Where lies the opportunity for consistency? *In our proclaimed positions!* Continue to stand against, rather than embrace and espouse, these errors with which we presently are compelled to live.[3]

Let only a few achieve enough understanding of how the free market works its wonders, along with the ability to explain the reasons, and the pre-emptors will fade into oblivion. Darkness always gives way to light. Similarly, the error of the Command Society has no resistance to the light and truth of the Free Society.

---

[3]"The Consistent Life." Copy on request from FEE.

8

THE VAGARIES
OF VALUE JUDGMENTS

*One cool judgment is worth a
thousand hasty councils.*
—WOODROW WILSON

Rereading my 1964 Journal recently, I came upon an all-but-forgotten letter. It was written to me by a man who is both rich and famous. Never have I been so overrated, and this puffery is perhaps one explanation as to why he fell by the wayside—no signs of a continuing interest. In any event, there was in this and similar cases a dramatic turnabout in value judgment—not at all uncommon—the reasons for which are worthy of examination. Here is the letter, slightly abbreviated:

This is first of all a "fan" letter, secondly, a thank you letter and lastly, it is a letter of transmittal. But one at a time.

Your recent work, *Anything That's Peaceful,* is great, outstanding, stupendous, elegant, everlasting, wonderful, magnificent, articulate and noble! Your 238 pages consolidate into an orderly philosophy all the many thoughts that a reader may previously have accumulated. Furthermore, those same pages present many new ideas, some shocking at first, but lovingly embraced when they turn out to be the missing links between segments of a partly assembled puzzle. You are truly a prophet. Today you may be heard only by the remnant, but your work embodies more truths than that of Adam Smith. It most surely will become a standard text for the generations who survive the fall of statism.

Thank you for sending me an autographed copy of *Anything That's Peaceful.* I read it slowly (over a ten day period), reread many passages, and when half way through, ordered five additional copies from FEE. I am grateful for your little gift of a single copy. But my real gratitude is for your wondrous works which have brought a new satisfaction, the satisfaction which comes from achieving a new level of understanding.

Enclosed are two checks for $10 and $28. . . . Please find another of my checks for $10,000, for whatever purpose The Foundation for Economic Education, Inc. may deem appropriate.

"Overrating" is a feeble term to describe the above. 'Tis a momentary idolatry, doubtless inspired by novel phrasings of his own ideas which excite him. Later, he comes to himself with the inevitable adverse reaction—a swing equally as far in the opposite direction. I have yet to observe an overrating that was not followed by a comparable underrating—a pendulum kind of action. Any time someone refers to himself as your disciple, prepare for a swing to the opposite appraisal. You, as "the god," turn to dust because of the mistaken presumption that you were a god in the first place! Henri-Frederic Amiel correctly observed:

If we begin by overrating the being we love, we shall end by treating it with wholesale injustice.

Interestingly, value judgments that begin with underrating another, seem never to result in overrating. What is the explanation? I can only hazard a guess based on what's happened to me. Countless times over the years I have discovered in others a wisdom that previously escaped my notice. Their quietude? My ineptitude? In any event, my gratitude! What happens is no change in them, only in me—my enlightenment. There is no place for overrating in this equation. It would be absurd to overrate my tiny enlightenment—or its sources!

A famous author comes to mind—an out-and-out atheist. As we say in air flight, he did a 180, becoming a devout Christian. No overrating is possible in his case or of The Source. Old and darkened vistas fade as Divine and glowing vistas come into view. Here is an example of a value judgment that graces the achiever.

What a brilliant observation by Woodrow Wilson: "One *cool* judgment is worth a thousand hasty councils." By "councils," he assuredly meant the same as Leo Tolstoy:

From the day when the first members of *councils* placed exterior authority higher than interior, that is to say, recognized the decisions of men united in councils as more important and more sacred than reason and conscience, on that day began the lies that caused the loss of millions of human beings and which continue their unhappy work to the present day.[1]

I feel equally certain that Wilson's phrase, "One cool judgment," was meant to convey the same thought as Tolstoy's "reason and conscience." At this point it is important to reflect on the distinction between councils and counsels.

Councils are committees reaching for the lowest common denominator. The truth as each individual discerns it—cool judgment—is forfeited for whatever most nearly approximates majority opinion. This is mere nose counting, which is nothing more than a mindless or senseless potpourri! As C. F. Kettering wisely observed, "If you want to kill any idea in the world today, get a committee working on it." We hear a lot about "environmental pollution" these days; we should be more concerned with the pollution spewing forth from councils.

Cool judgment goes hand in hand with an individual's concept of righteousness. This leads him to seek *counsel* from those who, in his opinion, may enlighten. After which he stands on his own two feet, as we say, making sure that his proclaimed positions are absolutely consistent with the truth as he sees it. Such a stance is a goal which any one of us might achieve.

Another reflection on the vagaries of value judgments.

---

[1]Leo Tolstoy, *The Law of Love and The Law of Violence* (New York: Rudolph Field, 1948), p. 26.

For further comments on councils, see "Appoint a Committee" in my *Anything That's Peaceful* (FEE, 1964), pp. 99-107. Also, "On Being My Own Man" in my *Castles in the Air*, pp. 93-98.

Cool judgments—reason and conscience—have an enormous force working against them, which is responsible for a gruesome distortion of the process of decision making. Instead of seeking counsel from those who enlighten, most people are guided by pomp and ceremony, by those in the limelight, that is, by persons in conspicuous positions before the public. It's the king-can-do-no-wrong syndrome.

Let a President of the U.S.A. advocate wage and price controls, or any one of countless other absurdities, and millions of people are afflicted with warped judgments. When the Queen of England confers the title of Lord on a Cambridge professor, who then tells the world that we can spend ourselves rich, the masses—including a large percentage of teachers—genuflect before the man-made Lord and his nonsense.

Let those who are skilled and famous in a single trade or science or art utter nonsense in areas beyond their competence, and millions bow the knee. Those who do no thinking for themselves will accept the word of the world's most renowned mathematician, for instance, on matters about which he knows nothing but is unaware of the fact. Thus, those who have not developed discriminatory talents stuff their heads with folly.

A concluding value judgment: The force which gives socialism the appearance of working is the freedom which socialism has not as yet been able to destroy. Give America a few *cool judgments* and we will know why freedom works its wonders!

9

IDLE WORDS

Every idle word that men shall speak, they shall give account thereof in the day of judgment.
—MATTHEW XII:36

Following a lecture of mine, a dozen or so people gathered around asking questions or seeking further explanation of this or that point. One man had something else on his mind. This gent, in disagreement with my freedom point of view, pretty much monopolized the time with heated argument— at once amusing and pitiful! I put this kind of an exchange in the category of idle words—for two reasons. First, I was not seeking light from him and, second, he kept the others from sharing such information as I might possess. To argue is nothing less than frivolity—futile verbiage! The following comment by Aldous Huxley sets the stage for this thesis:

Unrestrained and indiscriminate talk is morally evil and spiritually dangerous. . . . This may seem a very hard saying. And yet if we pass in review the words we have given vent to in the course of the average day, we shall find that the greater of them may be classified under three main heads: (1) words inspired by malice and uncharitable-

58

ness toward our neighbors; (2) words inspired by greed, sensuality and self-love; (3) words inspired by pure imbecility and uttered without rhyme or reason, but merely for the sake of making a distracting noise.

These are idle words; and we shall find, if we look into the matter, that they tend to outnumber the words that are dictated by reason, charity or necessity. And if the unspoken words of our mind's endless, idiot monologue are counted, the majority for idleness becomes, for most of us, overwhelmingly large.[1]

Let's make it clear at the outset that disagreement is in no way to be disparaged. As explained in a previous chapter, differences are blessings; they are the way to truth. My only point is that to lock horns in argument is not a seeking process but a stifling one; it is not a stimulus to learning. Argument hardens those who differ in their respective differences.

Aldous Huxley, I feel certain, would not exempt even himself from those who use idle words. Perhaps no person has silenced himself perfectly in this respect. "And if the unspoken words . . . are counted"—words we think to ourselves but do not speak or write—what idle worders all of us are! In order to reduce our own idle wording and to be less victimized by the idle words of others, why not a few examples of this corrupting verbiage—something to serve as a guideline?

In which behavioral department of life do we find idle words in greatest quantity? No two answers can be identical. It depends on the scope of one's views—narrow or

---

[1]*The Perennial Philosophy* (New York: Harper & Brothers, 1945), pp. 216-217.

otherwise—on the kinds of talk or writing that attracts or beguiles, on the quality of personal value judgments— shallow or improving. Thus, what follows is only my very uncertain ranking of sources in terms of their verbal density.

In today's world, as I see it, political babble tops the list. While there are a few notable and laudable exceptions in public office—statesmen—the vast majority of those who seek election pay not the slightest heed to what they believe to be righteous. They are guided by one criterion: what idle words will garner the most votes? Instead of standard-setters they are standard-*up*setters—the curse of our times.

The tragedy is that most voters cannot distinguish a statesman from a politician and, thus, the latter, with their promises of something-for-nothing, have an edge in any political contest. Then, to implement their degraded schemes—political nightmares—those politicans cultivate an enormous bureaucracy of a like-minded ilk. We have in this utter immorality—idle words—an explanation for the present drive down the road to serfdom!

Let us reflect on another fact. Those persons who cannot recognize as fallacious the idle words they hear or read are in precisely the same category as the users thereof. Idle words uttered are no less deplorable than idle words believed. Indeed, were there no believers, there would be no users!

What behavioral department ranks next in its capacity to spew forth idle words? Second to the political sector I'd place the public media—again, with a few notable exceptions. I am speaking of radio, TV, newspapers and magazines. By and large, these media have no criterion but the sensational, that which attracts countless millions of sensation seekers. Their aim is not to rake in the votes; it is to rake in the dollars and with truth as much disregarded as by conscienceless seekers of political office. Parenthetically, this is not to condemn the acquisition of either votes or dollars, but only the misleading and dishonest means often employed to garner votes or dollars.

Misleading? What goes on is fantastically distorted. If a plane crashes, that's "news." Nary a word about the millions of miles flown each day of the year in safety and comfort. Who wants to hear about the commonplace—the truth! If some big-name individual gets in trouble, it's headlined day in and day out. This has an appeal to the sensation seekers. Not a word about the literally trillions of honest, above-board, commendable transactions that occur daily in the U.S.A. Briefly, misfortunes are dramatically featured; our blessings, millions of times more numerous, are rarely mentioned. Idle words galore!

So we come upon another fact. Those persons who are sensation seekers are no less the perpetrators of idle words than are the sensational fabricators! Were there none of the former, the latter wouldn't exist—no dollars to rake in!

There are, of course, ever so many behavioral departments of life overburdened with idle words. The above two are but samplings of the most obvious. Now, for a commentary on an all but forgotten one and, thus, in today's world, the least obvious: prayer by rote. For evidence that this was once known, refer to Matthew VI:7: "But when ye pray, use not vain repetitions, as the heathens do."

What do the heathens vainly repeat? Wrote Reginald Heber in 1812: "The heathen in his blindness, bows down to wood and stone." This is by way of assessing what we observe more and more: obeisance repeatedly paid *only* to dollars, things, and the like—the material at the expense of the mental and the spiritual!

Those among us who are not heathens, the individuals who do in fact engage in daily prayers, are well advised to avoid prayer by rote—vain repetitions. Why vain? Prayer, or meditation, is intense mental action, and, to be meaningful, must have an appreciation of every word and thought. Otherwise, only idle words!

Is there a remedy for this idle-word syndrome? Indeed, there is: *Golden Silence!* This demands that we quiet *all* words—not just those that are spoken or written, but even those that are thought—forgo all words that are:

1. inspired by malice and uncharitableness toward our neighbors;
2. inspired by greed, sensuality and self-love;
3. inspired by pure imbecility and uttered without rhyme or reason, but merely for the sake of making distracting noise.

What then can be admitted into this silence to qualify it as Golden? As Huxley suggested, "words dictated by reason, charity or necessity." We think in words. Thus confine our thoughts to those which advance not only our own emergence in awareness, perception, consciousness, but a refining charitableness to our fellowmen. Golden Silence calls for an observation of the Golden Rule.

Finally, is Golden Silence attainable? Hardly, for such achievement would presuppose the perfect person. However, if we know what the road signs are, we can head in the right direction—idle words diminishing as we progress.

10

ARE YOU OUT
OF YOUR MIND?

*So many people who think they
have a tender heart have only a
soft mind.* —**JACQUES MARITAIN**

Are you out of your mind? This is a question each of us well
might ask that individual he sees in the mirror. Who me?
Yes, everyone! Why this confrontation? For a very good
reason: It is impossible for anyone to be quite sure how
much or how little knowledge there is in his finite mind.
Self-blindness leads to overassessments, and all
overassessments—notions that we know more than we
do—are *out* of mind, not in. This common affliction ranges
from slightly out of mind to nearly all out of mind.

Reflect on those who are only slightly out of mind, the
ones who do acknowledge mystery in all things. Mysterious
is the single atom; more so are the 30 trillion atoms which
could be placed on the period at the end of this sentence
without overlapping; and so much more mysterious are the
octillion atoms—1,000,000,000,000,000,000,000,000,000—
which compose one's body. Nearly everything is mystery,
from a blade of grass to galaxies receding into outer space at

the speed of light. But even those persons who bow so low and humbly before Infinite Intelligence are unable to escape some overassessment of what's in the mind. After all, man is imperfect—no exception.

At issue here, however, are those who so greatly overassess the contents of their mentality that they are really out of their minds and, not at all surprisingly, are unaware of the fact. Each of these is remindful of the shaman, or medicine man: "a man supposed to have supernatural powers of curing disease and controlling spirits." But such purveyors of spells are to be found everywhere, and not only in primitive tribes!

I recall medicine men at the county fairs when I was a lad in the early years of this century, their horse-drawn vans loaded with this or that bottled "life saver" claimed to cure every disease and ailment. What spellbinders—word charmers—they were! And awe-struck audiences, all that could crowd within range of their bewitching voices! Furthermore, those medicine men as firmly believed their incantations as do witch doctors. Out of their minds!

Who are today's medicine men? With rare exceptions, they are individuals so far out of their minds that they use or advocate *coercive force* as a means of casting the creative lives of the millions in the image of their infinitesimal selves. Such medicine men are to be found among those elected and appointed to public office, among those who preside over classrooms and religious congregations. Labor union officials are prone to such abuse of power, and so are business and professional men and women. Indeed, there is not an occupational category that is free of these perfectly absurd dictocrats.

Observe how similar are today's medicine men to those of the past. They actually believe that they have supernatural powers, enabling them to direct the creative activities of other people better than those folk can direct themselves! Most of them are artists of the spoken word. The awe-struck audiences flock around, not by the dozens, but by the millions! Today's medicine men believe their incantations to be truth no less than did the witch doctors of yore.

However, medicine men today differ from witch doctors and those of my boyhood in one striking respect. The salesman of the "magic elixir" from the rear of his horse-drawn van had a single trick to cast his spell over small audiences: to charm them with words! Contemporary medicine men? True, they include verbal hocus-pocus but they are not satisfied with the few who might be seduced by that alone. So, what do they add? *Coercion!* No freedom to choose whether to buy their medicine or not? It's do as they say or else!

Before going further, let me emphasize the point of this thesis: the extent to which anyone, in or out of political office, uses or advocates *coercion* to get his way, to that extent is he a modern medicine man—out of his mind![1] Wrote Herbert Spencer:

That which fundamentally distinguishes the slave is that he labours under *coercion* to satisfy another's desires.

That brilliant author of *The Man Versus the State,* and many other books—hard-headed and plain spoken—used *coercion,* a term rarely written or spoken in his or our country

[1]Coercion is aggressive as distinguished from defensive force. For a detailed explanation, see *Accent on the Right* (FEE, 1968), pp. 43-44.

today. I had to refer to his nation's *The Oxford Dictionary* to find the explanation:

> As the word has, in later times, a bad flavour, *suggesting the application of force as a remedy* . . . it is now usually avoided by those who approve of the action in question.

The action in question? Any one of countless proposals to obtain special privilege by law: legal edicts backed by physical force—the constabulary. Every aspect of the planned economy and the welfare state falls in this category. These range from compulsory seat belts to food stamps; from minimum wages to maximum hours; from tariffs, embargoes, quotas to all restrictions of competition and freedom in transactions; from government education to getting paid for not farming or not working; from social security to medicare to—you name it! That is, if you can live long enough!

Bear in mind that the advocacy of force—whether from classroom or pulpit or wherever, whether against neighbor or neighborhood or country—is no less a part of "the action in question" than the actual practice of force. Advocacy is cause, practice is effect. Merely estimate the number of us who "labour under *coercion* to satisfy another's desires" and there will be the extent of slavery in the U.S.A. today. It defies calculation!

Very well! Why "the bad flavour" of *coercion?* There is hardly a person among the millions who advocate or practice "the action in question" who cares to think of himself as that kind of a culprit. Personally, of course not! However, let the action be not in one's own name but camouflaged by a collective label—society, government, democracy, or whatever—and a false absolution comforts all who are out of their minds, who "think" how hunky-dory all would be were all the likes of me!

Is it any wonder that the term *coercion* is avoided like the plague! "Bad flavour," indeed! And that's precisely the "flavour" it should have. Why not call coercionists by the right name? And that should include ourselves, if the term befits us!

"So many people who think they have a tender heart have only a soft mind." What a wise observation not only of our times but of every devolutionary period throughout history! This is to say, be kind to those in distress, not with one's own loaf of bread, but with bread coercively taken from others. In these cases, the hearts are tender enough but the minds are soft. Out of their minds and out of other people's pockets—by coercion! When one's heart is tender and the mind not soft, what is the behavior? He shares his own, not someone else's loaf with those in distress. Judeo-Christian charity is actually extravagant when the concern for others is not pre-empted by coercive practices!

Were legalized coercion to receive its support only from its true believers, that is, from such open and proud exponents as Karl Marx, Earl Browder, Norman Thomas, and the like, that absurd way of life wouldn't have a "ghost of a chance," as the saying goes. Who then supplies the drive? *The exception makers!* I am for the free society *but* in education we must have compulsory attendance, government dictated curricula, and the forcible collection of the wherewithal to pay the bills! *But* we must have wage and price controls! *But* people would starve without food stamps and social security! *Buts* on and on and on!

To cite an example, the best freedom devotee in all of Austria once said to me, "I find myself so emotionally committed to the Vienna Opera (state owned) that in this instance I must make an exception." In a word, Austrians—even those who care not one whit for opera—must be coerced into paying for those who adore opera. This example by my good friend inspired me to write an article, "Sinking In a Sea of Buts."[2]

Based on a wide acquaintance all over our country for many years, it is my guess that not less than 99 per cent of adult Americans have one or more *buts*. Here lies the source of the mess we're in—millions out of their minds, more or less. My counsel: Watch your *buts*, buddy!

A word of encouragement: but—this is my *but*—the situation is less hopeless than it appears to be. Why? Thank heaven, this out-of-your-mind malady is not a numbers problem. Were it a matter of a majority coming to themselves, attaining a realization of how little really is in the mind—no chance!

The requirement? Let only a few, a tiny minority, see the utter nonsense of coercion as a means of satisfying one's own or another's desires—making slaves of all—and the medicine men will become impotent. No more than a small beam of light will put coercionists to shame, a bright glare they will fear to face. To whom should you and I look for this restoration of common sense? To that only person for whom you and I are responsible: the one viewed in the mirror!

---

[2]See *The Freeman,* April 1970.

11

HERDED, OR HEADED ONE'S OWN WAY?

The ideal society would enable every man and woman to develop along their individual lines, and not attempt to force all into one mould, however admirable.
—JOHN HALDANE

An ideal society should, indeed, be so framed that you are free to head your way along the lines of your uniqueness, and I am free to head my way. This is to say, neither you nor I should be *herded*—forced into a common mould. Excellent thinking, John Haldane, but I wonder what you meant by "however admirable"!

Anyone who understands the ideal society, as did this Englishman, could not possibly admire any one of countless common moulds into which dictocrats are attempting to force unique human beings. He had too much respect for you and me to call such political hocus-pocus "admirable." To what, then, was he referring?

In all likelihood, Haldane was speaking ironically of Communism, Socialism, or similar schemes for secular salvation. These utopian visions are pipe-dreams—vain hopes, fantastic ideas, impossible plans. There are millions of pipe-dreamers in the U.S.A. today, and no two dream alike. Each believes his dream to be "admirable," and is as certain of his self-proclaimed utopia as was Karl Marx, one of the most notorious and discredited—but nevertheless influential—pipe-dreamers of all time.

Such dreamers are victims of a mental depravity—a messianic complex. I'm reminded of the chap in the cartoon, paying his psychiatrist and remarking, "You call this a cure? When I came to you, I was Napoleon, and now I'm nobody."

Perhaps "Napoleonitis" best identifies this disease. These dreamers sincerely regard as admirable their schemes to herd us into a common mould—their moulds, each different. Interestingly, a vast majority of them are highly "educated." They interpret their years of "schooling" and graduation as certifying a high level of wisdom and, thus, are infatuated with their prowess. The truth is that life— every mortal moment—is, at best, *commencement*. Like the rest of us, they know next to nothing. But they are unaware of their limitations, and this may explain their insistence on domineering over you and me, of herding us into their "admirable" moulds.

Why are these pipe-dreams—most of them—"vain hopes," authoritarian schemes impossible of fulfillment? In the first place, there are so many—literally millions—that no government official or private citizen has ever heard of more than a fraction of them. We've all heard of seat belts, for the manufacturers have been compelled to install them, but reflect on the large percentage of drivers and passengers who choose not to tie themselves to their seats.

We had to install a new toilet at FEE. The plumber said it was illegal to use an oval seat, that a U-shaped seat had to be used in all public toilets. Is this a local, state, or national law? Who knows! It's a safe guess that no pipe-dreamer can answer the question. And were one to research the matter—who cares!—I'll wager that the violations would be impressive. And it's anyone's guess as to how many millions of other pipe-dreams have been made the law of the land.[1]

Of course, there's another reason why pipe-dreams are vain hopes, even when known: people ignore them. A minor example: The enormous disregard of laws prohibiting the bringing of cigarettes and liquor from some states where they're less taxed to one's own state where taxes are higher. Many citizens, from all walks of life, become law breakers, black market operators, smugglers. They'll course around countless pipe-dreams and the consequence is a massive moral degeneration.

Some concluding reflections on the know-nothing-ness of pipe-dreamers:

- Knowing not how to prohibit various iniquities, they tend to legalize them.
- Knowing not how to prevent thievery, they do the taking themselves.
- Knowing not how to identify or prevent inflation, they inflate the money supply.
- Knowing not how to suppress labor violence, they give it their coercive support.

---

[1]For an interesting article on other pipe-dreams less gross than toilet seats, see "The Age of the Technicality" by Clarence Carson. *The Freeman,* March 1976.

- Knowing not how to inhibit aggression among citizens, they become aggressors themselves.
- Knowing not how to invoke a common justice, they perpetrate injustices.
- Knowing not how to run their own lives, they dream up schemes to run ours.

The pipe-dreamers have this much going for them: they are in great demand. Millions of people prefer being herded to finding their own way. Do their own politico-economic thinking? Perish such a perplexing thought! They prefer that others do such thinking for them, especially when this carries promises of easy welfare. Unable to identify false promises, they become the victims of their own shallow envy and greed. That is, unless rescued by those few who have found their own heading.

In reflecting on the few who are headed their own way, I recalled this impressive quatrain from the *Rubáiyát of Omar Khayyám:*

> And that inverted Bowl they call the Sky,
> Whereunder crawling coop'd we live and die,
>   Lift not your hand to *It* for help—for It
> As impotently moves as you and I.

Ralph Bradford, whose many talents include setting ideas to verse, has paraphrased it for me:

> And are you then so weak and self-forsaken
> You turn for succor to the vast but shaken
>   And barren branches of the State? Beware!
> It cannot give a thing it has not taken!

Those who think for themselves, who are headed their

own way, know full well that government cannot feather the nests of some except at the expense of others—all the political babble to the contrary notwithstanding! Knowing this is a first step in heading one's own way.

The second step is suggested by Margaret Cameron in her book, *The Seven Purposes:*

> Give unto each his opportunity to grow and to build for progress. Freedom to strive is the one right inherent in existence, the strong and the weak each following his own creative purpose, with all his force, to the one great end. *And he who binds and limits his brother's creative purpose binds himself now and hereafter.* But he who *extends* his brother's opportunity, builds for eternity.

How does one *extend* his brother's opportunity? By pursuing one's own uniqueness, tending to one's own knitting, growing in one's creativity and never, under any circumstance, standing in the creative path of his brother. And never lending one's sanction when governments do so—be they Federal, state, or local.

Away with herding into common moulds! Let every man and woman develop along their individual lines—each heading his or her own creative way. Such would be freedom: *the ideal society!*

12

HOW MEASURE GROWTH?

The student of history must avoid
that error which the proverb calls
measuring other people's corn by
one's own bushel. —**E. B. TYLOR**

A correspondent from Pakistan asked: "How can one tell whether a nation is experiencing economic growth?" A bit of reflection brought this thought: Really, a nation experiences no more than a corn crib; *only individuals have experiences.* So, if we would measure progress—or regress—it must be with respect to individual human beings, never a nation.

One of the Bicentennials being celebrated in 1976 is Adam Smith's *Wealth of Nations.* This great moral philosopher should not be blamed for allowing the line of collectivists, tracing through Marx and Keynes, to prolong the myth of national wealth and material income most commonly designated today as the Gross National Product (GNP). But the Bicentennial could well serve as occasion to examine those ideas.

Any individual's economic wealth is generally expressed as his net worth, and changes in net worth show how much he is gaining or losing in wealth.

As to nations, some are more economically advanced than others, and a major reason for the difference is the degree of freedom exercised by individuals to the point that capital is accumulated and put to productive use. Real wages tend to be higher in countries with the most savings invested per worker. But this is most likely to happen where private ownership and control of property is respected and upheld through limited government—where there is freedom to trade in open competition—where prices are free to fluctuate in response to supply and demand in the unhampered market—where the money to facilitate trade is left to the market rather than printed by government to serve political purposes—where charity is personal and private as distinguished from welfare state plundering of the productive to subsidize the wastrels—where entrepreneurial response to change and opportunity is encouraged rather than frustrated and forbidden.

It is true that in a free market economy there is no need for any such measurement as GNP or national wealth or full employment or percent of income taken in taxes. All that is needed is the information freely available to every potential buyer and seller in the form of market prices. Individuals and businesses can act intelligently on the basis of that information. They have no need for and should be free to ignore whatever GNP or other statistics governments want to assemble.

I can't get very excited about the fact that such statistics are gathered and published. But if they are being used in such a way as to interfere with personal choices and actions—which they are—that is serious and should be explained.

In taking this position, I find myself in contention with Hegel, Marx, Comte, and many of our own time, who embrace the notion that only the nation or society is real and that the individual is the abstraction. Today, these socialist sophists have followers by the millions, collectivists who are but copycats of ancient and medieval forms of coercion—those who favor a Charlemagne, Napoleon, Hitler, or in today's terms, the planned economy and the welfare state.

Summarized, the argument is between those who pose society or the nation as the prime unit and those of us who believe that all meaningful comparisons in progress or regress must be made in terms of individual or business units.

Conceded, the problem of measuring growth is partly an accounting problem, but the measurement, to make sense, has to do with the unit in question, be the unit an individual or company. Each unit has different goals, values, aspirations, ambitions. Thus, there can be no single measuring rod for social or national or collective growth.

In the free market each unit does its own calculating. This is known as economic calculation—business accounting—determination of profit or loss. It is this that leaves each unit free to choose what to produce, what and with whom to exchange, and what to buy or consume.

Dr. Ludwig von Mises was the first to demonstrate the impossibility of economic calculation under socialism.[1] Economic calculation is automatically supplied in a system of free competitive pricing. Leading communist

---

[1] *Socialism* (New Haven: Yale University Press, 1951), pp. 131-42.

"economists" concede his point. Their words, my italics:

> The best methods of producing a given output cannot be chosen [by socialist methods] but are taken from outside the [socialist] system . . . i.e. methods of production used in the past, or so-called "advanced" methods of production, *usually taken from the practice of more advanced countries and used as data for plan-building by the* [socialist] *country under consideration.*[2]

As more and more countries, including the United States, succumb to socialism, upon what information are the communist "economists"—or anyone, for that matter—to base their plans? Upon the GNP? Wrote Henry Hazlitt of this political fantasy:

> It is impossible . . . to arrive at a precise, scientific, objective, or absolute measurement of the national income in terms of dollars. But the assumption that we *can* do so has led to dangerous policies, *and threatens to lead to even more dangerous policies.*[3]

It is the catastrophic situation into which an acceptance of GNP leads that warrants—indeed, demands—our examination.

The countless little Caesars who man our present socialistic structure have decisions to make. Economic calculation is impossible under socialism. Their single recourse? Statistics! Wrote Murray Rothbard:

> Statistics are, in a crucial sense, critical to all interventionist and socialistic activities of government. . . . Only

---

[2]*The Journal of the American Economic Association,* March, 1963.
[3]*The Failure of the "New Economics"* (Princeton: D. Van Nostrand Co., Inc., 1960), p. 415.

by statistics can the Federal government make even a
fitful attempt to plan, regulate, control, or reform various
industries—or impose central planning and socialization
on the entire economic system.[4]

To the extent that an economy is controlled by government, it is no longer a reflection of freedom of choice and
competitive forces but rather of bureaucratic edicts. These
edicts decree this or that according to the statistical data
which they compile. While numerous data are contrived for
their use, the usual statistic for measuring economic growth
is gross national product: GNP. Absurd?

- If a man divorces his wife and hires her as a cook at $50
  a week, the GNP will increase by $2,600 annually.
- The dollars paid farmers not to grow crops boost the
  GNP as do the dollars paid farmers for things produced.

It is useless to give other examples, for the input statistical "guidelines" are forever changing, not only with the
passing whims of each dictocrat but also with the whims of
the others as they come and go. This explains why there is
so little agreement on what GNP really is. I don't know;
they don't know!

Only this we know for certain: GNP—always expressed
in the monetary unit—enlarges whenever the medium of
exchange is diluted; that is, GNP expands in an inflationary
period. Contemplate what Germany's GNP was in 1923
when billions of marks wouldn't buy a loaf of bread! GNP
reached its peak just before total collapse!

In view of its absurdity, why is GNP employed as a
measuring rod? When economic calculation—automatic in

---

[4]"Statistics: Achilles' Heel of Government," *The Freeman,* June 1961.

competitive pricing—is rejected, errors follow as a consequence. At least, GNP is consistent with the absurd premise of the interventionists: the notion that they can run our lives better than we can. How can they be expected to know there isn't any measuring rod!

Further, interventionists naively believe in the Keynesian notion that increased government expenditures lead to prosperity. Were this true, we should repeal the laws against counterfeiting. The fact? Exploding government expenditures foretell catastrophe, nothing else.

Here is a rarely understood fact: Free market performances do not lend themselves to mathematical analysis any more than do intellectual, moral and spiritual values. This is to say that the economic status of individuals cannot be measured by any objective standard—none whatsoever! Statistics are nonsensical—Achilles' heel, indeed.

National objective standards—devices of the dictocrats—are, of course, erroneous. What then for a free society? *Subjective judgments!* This is not to say that the individual can have no awareness of his own economic improvement; it is only to assert that such growth cannot be reckoned by any objective standard.

For instance, *what I want to do* is forever changing and *what I want in exchange* is like a bird on the wing—I don't stay put. More to the point, no two human beings are alike; all of us are in flux, not only as individuals but relative to each other.

It so happens that my highest aspiration is to write and lecture on behalf of the freedom way of life. I prefer this to other employments, even though the other jobs available may pay ever so much more. And in exchange I desire above all else a working acquaintance with the best of freedom thinkers in the world, along with the economic means—food, transportation, and the like—for realization. To me, this is the ultimate in progress. Who has any right to set a standard for me other than these unusual but nonetheless self-chosen goals? Not a person on this earth!

But here's another fellow who, above all else, prefers to strum a guitar. And in exchange his heart's desire is "a Loaf of Bread . . . a Flask of Wine, a Book of Verse—and Thou." To him this is the ultimate in progress. Where is the superman who has any logical, moral, or ethical basis for decreeing otherwise? No such person exists or ever will!

The above gets at the crux of the matter: evaluation of progress is individual and subjective; gain or loss cannot be objectively measured; that is, neither I nor anyone else can devise a standard that can accurately assess what is or isn't a gain to any other.

What is progress to one individual may very well be regress to another. Examples: There are persons who would prefer an audience with the President of the U.S.A. to $10,000, and vice versa; a hoola hoop to $5, and vice versa; a Ph.D. to $5,000, and vice versa—and so on ad infinitum. *Objective standards simply cannot be used to measure subjective judgments!* GNP is a fraud, in most instances an innocent one! No freedom devotee should ever refer to it except disapprovingly.

When we discover that each of us is unique and is the best judge and master of his own growth, we will try to so structure our society that freedom of choice is maximized— liberty for one and all.

13

IDOLIZING ERROR

*Nothing is more harmful to a new
truth than an old error.*

—GOETHE

The question is this: Should we devotees of liberty present
both sides, that is, the side of liberty on the one hand and the
side of slavery on the other? This is a common notion,
supported and advocated by teachers, preachers, politicians, ever so many businessmen, and others.

I contend that, historically speaking, liberty is a brand
new truth and slavery is an old error. Nearly everyone in
our country today thinks of slavery as something practiced
prior to the Civil War—a Simon Legree-Negro relationship.
True, that suggests "a relentless taskmaster," but serious
reflection reveals that the definition also applies to numerous human relationships in our day.

Let me illustrate with reference to an act by the Roman
Emperor, Domitian (A.D. 51-96). Like all despots, then and
now, Domitian suffered an abysmal ignorance parading as
infinite wisdom. In his "wisdom" he exiled a slave—one
Epictetus. Yet, so brilliant was this slave's light that it
mirrored its way for more than fifteen centuries through
such philosophers as Grotius, Kant, Adam Smith, Adam
Ferguson, and many more.

81

History affords no better example of despotic action to stifle creative genius by one who knows not what he does. Bear in mind that all human creativity begins as a hidden potentiality in some person unknown. Indeed, that individual himself cannot foresee his creative spark. Epictetus, the slave, did not. The newsboy, Tom Edison, had no idea that he was to become a great inventive genius. Examples, if known, should include the cave dweller who discovered how to harness fire, the Hindu who invented the concept of zero, on and on and on.

The fact is that the despots—Domitian, or his counterparts today—cannot direct creativity; they can only stifle it. They are not wise enough to handle a power of coercion over others. Nor will anyone ever be!

Now, it seems obvious that we must have an agency of society that inhibits the destructive actions of men, one that codifies the taboos and enforces them, leaving all of us free to act creatively as we please. This is what is meant by *limited* government. The opposite and evil use of force is when politicians and bureaucrats aggress, that is, when they use the force of government in an effort to cast us in their images. This is what I mean by coercion, for I believe that aggression against other human beings and the coercing of them is one and the same evil action—enslavement.

Compulsory seat belts exemplify this evil action— freedom of choice denied. On occasion, a person falls out of bed or off his chair. Why not compulsory bed belts or chair belts? Too absurd? No more so than the thousand and one other commonly accepted coercive actions which inhibit the freedom of anyone to act creatively as he pleases. The distinction between a bed belt and a tariff or any other form of coercive protectionism is that the absurdity is more easily discerned in the former. Each is a blow to liberty—freedom of choice. The same can be said for all infractions of the free market and private ownership way of life.

"Government can't give us anything without depriving us of something else," is the way Henry Hazlitt puts it in his article, "Instead of What?" in the March 1976 *Freeman*.

> . . . practically all these subsidy measures, all these schemes to redistribute income or to force Peter to support Paul, are one-eyed as well as shortsighted. They get their immediate appeal by focusing attention on the alleged needs of some particular group of intended beneficiaries. But the inevitable victims—those who are going to be asked to pay for the new handout in increased taxes (which directly or indirectly means almost everybody else)—are left out of account.
>
> Only one-half of the problem has been seen. The cost of the proposed solution has been overlooked.

An aside: there is no known phase of human action that the coercionists have not attempted to bring under their control. Why then, by this time, are we not wholly enslaved? *It is the unknown,* the hidden creativity in countless thousands of individuals, often stimulated more by adversity than by prosperity. Thank God that no political dictocrat is efficient enough to plug all loopholes.

Today's coercionist—the political dictocrat—is as much to be deplored as Domitian or Simon Legree. One is just as much "a relentless taskmaster" as the other.

I repeat Herbert Spencer's truth, "That which fundamentally distinguishes the slave is that he labours under coercion to satisfy another's desires." Does it matter whether he labors in Simon Legree's cotton field in exchange for next to nothing or labors for high earnings only to have them taxed away to satisfy the demands of countless millions who produce nothing at all? This pack of parasites includes the coercionists who stimulate and develop these unwarranted demands.

Bastiat referred to this mode of social conduct as legal plunder:

> See if the law takes from some persons what belongs to them, and gives it to other persons to whom it does not belong. See if the law benefits one citizen at the expense of another by doing what the citizen himself cannot do without committing a crime.

The present-day coercionist, no less than Domitian, is a despot who enslaves others.

Why this emphasis on the evil of slavery? I am unaware of any error more at odds with human destiny—emergence, evolution, growth in consciousness. In the practice of slavery, we have finite minds parading as Infinite Wisdom. To me, slavery—man's denial of freedom—tops the list of all human errors and leads to many of the others.

Why, then, do we idolize this error and persist in the practice of slavery? It is the tug of tradition, the continuation of primitive ways—unless reason comes to the rescue. As John Locke observed: "Habits work more constantly and with greater force than reason, which, when we have most need of it, is seldom fairly consulted, and more rarely obeyed." Thus, we seem to have always with us the relentless taskmasters, past and present. Reason has not yet come to their rescue—or ours.

In contrast to the old habit of slavery, liberty is a brand new truth. This new idea—freedom of choice; no man-concocted restraints against the release of creative human energy—began to emerge 200 years ago with the simultaneous appearance of Adam Smith's *Wealth of Nations,* and the *American Declaration of Independence.* To most people, anything born two centuries ago is old hat. What possibly could be brand new about a truth that aged?

Admittedly, we cannot see into the future—foresight—and few of us have the faculty accurately to assess the past—hindsight. We live in years, not centuries, and the present looms large in our thinking. We do not see ourselves and our times in proper perspective. And what is really brand new may appear to be quite ancient—or vice versa.

To help remedy such shortsightedness, construct a calendar of life on earth, collapsing eons of time into a single year, a comprehensible time span.

In January through August there were traces of life. The first insects appeared in October; in November arrived the first reptiles, dinosaurs, crocodiles, mammals; in December, the first snakes, flowering plants, elephants, deer.

It was shortly after 7:00 P.M. on December 31 that man appeared—in the glacial period. As midnight approached—only 10 minutes to go—Cro-Magnon man put in an appearance.

11:58	the beginning of recorded history
11:58:30	the first civilization (Sumer)
11:59:15	Athens in her glory
11:59:29	The birth of Christ
11:59:51.5	Columbus discovered America

But note this: Just 3½ seconds before midnight appeared *The Wealth of Nations* and the *Declaration of Independence*.

Liberty is, indeed, a brand new *truth*!

Having tried to make plain what slavery is and why so many people persist in this dreadful error, I return to the opening question: Should we, the devotees of liberty, present both sides: Must we, in order "to be fair," give equal time to slavery and liberty? Should we give the case for slavery, which we know to be false, the same platform dignity that we give to liberty?

I side with Hughston McBain: "If the evidence clearly indicates that an idea or policy is untrue or evil, no fair and objective person will voluntarily arrange to have it presented as valid."

My formula: Expose the error of slavery with all the talent one can bring to bear. And as to liberty, there is no need to defend this truth; it can stand by itself. I would simply *praise* it to high Heaven!

14

FREEDOM TO CHOOSE— BUT WHAT?

Between two evils, choose neither; between two goods, choose both. —**TYRON EDWARDS**

I, along with many others, have defined liberty over and over again as *freedom of choice*. By this we have meant that each individual should be free to choose his employment, to price his offerings of goods and services, to decide how the fruits of his labor shall be expended, to exchange what and with whom he pleases, and so on. However, it is just beginning to dawn on me that choice—choosing—has numerous interpretations other than mine. So, here is my attempt at refinement.

As a start, I would modify Tyron Edwards' sage advice to read: "Reject all that is evil; respect all that is good."

What are the few great evils? They are set forth in the Ten Commandments and include: Thou shalt not kill; Thou shalt not bear false witness; Thou shalt not covet; Thou shalt not steal. To examine one of these evils—stealing—should suffice to explain why it is best to reject what is evil and to choose what is good.

A Robinsoe Crusoe, of course, has no one to steal from. But let others appear in the territory and there is a network of relationships. This is *a society,* the persons in it being at once individualistic and social beings. The problem of what is mine and what is thine immediately arises. Stealing becomes possible. The moment anyone claims any scarce and valuable item there arises the question as to whether others will respect such claims or try to steal the property. Respect for private property leads to specialization and trade, the basis for a peaceful and prosperous society.

But what shall we say about stealing, beyond saying it's wrong? In the first place, a thief experiences no net gain—regardless of how great the loot he garners, and even if not caught. Admittedly, this is contrary to *his* warped judgment, even to popular opinion. If he is caught, a jail sentence would be the least of the penalties visited upon him. He suffers the loss of respect by his fellow men—ostracism—for who will engage in free exchange with a thief? But reflect on the penalty if not caught: the destruction of his soul—life's purpose enormously dulled. He who steals is his own worst enemy!

Can the term "free exchange" be applied to the relationship between a thief and his victim? Obviously not! A person is free to choose an evil act as well as a good one, but to choose theft is to violate freedom and to practice plunder! To grasp this point, one needs only to recognize that each of us is in society and, thus, each is, in this respect, a social being. Freedom is, therefore, a dual relationship; my freedom depends on yours and vice versa.

It should be self-evident that every act of theft—coercion of any sort—is a denial of freedom. Were the thief intelligent—a fanciful assumption—he would say of his acts: "I elect to feather my own nest at the expense of others by coercion and cheating. I have no respect for property rights; I repudiate the freedom of others to choose or reject free exchange. Others are not my equal, with rights to be respected; they are but sources for me to plunder."

It is a fair guess that nearly all Americans frown on the common thief—he who feathers his nest at the expense of others. But an equally fair guess is that these same "righteous" citizens are feathering their nests—wholly or partially—at the expense of others. One more guess: All the loot garnered in the private practice of theft is but a tiny fraction of that taken in our annual political sweepstakes for the purpose of redistributing wealth.

That the thief resorts to coercion—hidden or open—is self-evident. Yet, so do the millions of "innocents"—those who are unaware that their government "grants" are derived by the same malicious method. The special privilege any of us receives from government is forcefully taxed away from some rightful owner. Examples in the United States today are so numerous that no one can count them. They range from paying farmers not to grow crops to subsidizing other people's hospital bills to paying higher prices for goods and services by reason of labor union coercive tactics, protective tariffs, and similar interventions on behalf of persons or groups.

If the common thief is regarded as a rogue, then why don't the millions who feed at the government trough think of themselves as such? Rarely does anyone bother to question what "everybody is doing." But the more widespread the practice, the more important to ask: "Why do they do it?" For more reasons than I shall ever know, but here are several:

- The tug of tradition; Serfdom, Feudalism, Mercantilism, and the like. Our "planned economy" and "welfare state" are only new labels for old and accepted ways of politico-economic plundering.
- When celebrated individuals—those with big titles like *Lord* John Maynard Keynes, for instance—insist that we can spend ourselves rich, a something-for-nothing way of life, those who do no thinking for themselves accept this nonsense. They steal far more than common thieves, while entertaining the notion that they are helping their victims!
- "Men, it has been well said, think in herds; it will be seen that they go mad in herds, while they only recover their senses slowly, and one by one."[1]
- Enforced mediocrity! Politicians who look only to the next election, as contrasted to statesmen who look to oncoming generations, force their know-nothingness on the millions, most of whom welcome this relief from self-responsibility. Instead of rising to the challenge of competition, men are drawn down by the false lure of something for nothing.

In the above I have defined the evil in order to reject it. Now I shall pay my respects to what is good, so that *I* may choose the good. Why "I" and not "we"? I believe that everyone—no exception—should be free to act creatively as he or she chooses, and that I am endowed with no command over anyone else, nor would I accept it if offered. The single

---

[1]See *Extraordinary Popular Delusions and the Madness of Crowds* by Charles Mackay, LL.D. (New York: The Noonday Press, 1969).

person over whom I choose to have power is yours truly—
the power to expand my own creativity!

On what is this belief in individual responsibility founded?
Each human being is unique, no two remotely alike.[2] Indeed, no one of us stays put; creatively we either deteriorate
or expand from moment to moment. Further, there has
never been an instance of creativity expanded by force or
command. Rather, creativity flowers exclusively from free
will which, according to my dictionary, is "the human will
regarded as free from restraints, compulsions; freedom of
decision or choice."[3]

Above all, what in the realm of this thesis is good? It is
enlightened *self*-interest: attending to one's *own* creative
expansion. If at all successful, this evolving is, according to
the brilliant Frederic Bastiat, ". . . so illuminating, so
constant, and so penetrating, *when it is left free of hin-
drance.*" Thus, brighten one's own light and, if bright
enough, those who seek light will see it; they will choose the
good. Of course, freely share with those who care!

To see the good that I may choose the good requires a
recognition not only of my *skimpy wisdom* but, also, of
everyone else's finitude. To compare my finite consciousness to Infinite Consciousness as an atom to a galaxy would
be a gross exaggeration! Each separate ego is infinitesimal,
and all are different. Were everyone identical to any "I"—
Socrates, you, me, or anyone who lives—all would perish.
A moment's reflection and this is self-evident.

[2]See *You Are Extraordinary* by Roger J. Williams (New York: Random
House, 1967).

[3]Opponents of freedom will claim that there is creativity in Russia. There
is! But it is a leakage of creative energy. Can I command you to invent
something? Absurd!

Very well! the required awareness is within the range of anyone capable of thinking for self. Each of us is unique; everyone has a tiny bit of expertise at this or that, and there are as many variations as there are human beings.

How then do I best live, grow, prosper, move in the direction of my unrealized potentialities? Choose the good—freedom! This allows me to do anything I choose that is peaceful and allows all others the same. The benefit to be derived? I will serve others with whatever expertise I possess, and their uniqueness will serve me. As set forth in the beginning, this is what I mean by freedom of choice.

In this manner, may we be servants of all *and servile to none*!

15

PROMISES MEN DO AND DO NOT LIVE BY

Every civilization rests on a set of promises. . . . If the promises are broken too often the civilization dies. . . . **—HERBERT AGAR**

It would take nothing less than a book to explain the promises men live by. Indeed, Harry Scherman wrote such a book—481 pages—using that very title.[1] The set of promises on which civilization rests is rooted in integrity: borrow money, pay it back; make a contract, keep it; offer a good or service. let the representation of it be honest; make an engagement, respect it; title an article or book or sermon in accord with its content—on and on, no falsification whatsoever. These are the promises men live by.

My purpose here, however, is not to reflect on promises which are kept, but on those which are broken. Broken promises are enormously on the increase in the U.S.A. and

---

[1]See *The Promises Men Live By* by Harry Scherman (New York: Random House, 1939).

this bodes ill for our civilization. As a starter, here's an interesting thought from the Babylonian *Talmud:*

> The righteous promise little and perform much; the wicked promise much and perform not even a little.

There are, of course, numerous yardsticks for measuring those who are righteous and those who are wicked, the yardstick in this instance relating only to promises and performances. This Hebrew observation, written 15 centuries ago, measures men by what they do, not by what they say. Those who promise little and perform much are praised, while those who promise much and perform not even a little are condemned. Such a yardstick, applied to our day and age, makes a lot of sense. Indeed, it made sense to William Graham Sumner who, 14 centuries later—1883— wrote a masterpiece, *What Social Classes Owe to Each Other.*[2]

Sumner, a Professor of Political and Social Science at Yale University, clearly perceived an evil way of life taking root, one which has proliferated by leaps and bounds during the last forty years. "The forgotten man" was his label for the righteous. The wicked? Those reformers and social doctors—in and out of office—who advocate and employ the coercive force of government to subsidize nonworkers with the fruits of the forgotten man's labor.

False promises and the social doctors or reformers labeled as wicked! Performances and the forgotten man identified as righteous! Here is a ray of politico-economic light that has mirrored its way through the ages, seen by a

---

[2]*What Social Classes Owe to Each Other* by William Graham Sumner (Caldwell, Idaho: The Caxton Printers, Ltd., 1961).

few—our Founding Fathers and other intellectual stalwarts such as Sumner—and encouragingly on the increase. Civilizations rise and fall as the few perceive or fail to perceive this truth.

The masses, those who do no thinking for themselves and who range from paupers to millionaires, have forever been the victims of empty promises—the more extravagant, the greater the allure. Promise "All this and Heaven too!" if one's ambition be popularity, a mass following, millions genuflecting before the overesteemed self.

It is this mass deception which accounts for the false promisers: witch doctors, dictocrats, do-as-I-say reformers, be-like-me egotists. Nonthinkers—blind followers—constitute the target of these Pied Pipers. Thus the genesis of those who "promise much and perform not even a little."

It is easy to see why they promise much. But why do they perform "not even a little"? It is because the promises they make are *absolutely* impossible of fulfillment! They promise, for instance, to assure welfare to one and all, not with their substance but with yours and mine. The welfare rolls grow as the sources of funds diminish, until finally—all parasites and no hosts! The poor get poorer, the community goes bankrupt. Promises galore, performance nil!

The Pied Pipers promise more than welfare; they promise to plan the economy. Why, in this planned redistributive nonsense, do they perform "not even a little"? F. A. Hayek suggests the answer:

The chief reason why we cannot hope by central direction [government planning] to achieve anything like the efficiency in the use of resources which the market makes possible is that the economic order of any large society *rests on the utilization of the knowledge of particular circumstances widely dispersed among thousands or millions of individuals.*[3]

Even the millions who haven't the slightest idea of what makes an economy fruitful or unfruitful do, nonetheless, come up with literally trillions of goods and services—all novel and beneficial to millions of us whom they have no intention of benefiting. These unintentional benefactors are nudged into productivity not by politico-economic understanding. Far from it! What then? Adam Smith wrote the answer 200 years ago:

By directing that industry in such a manner as its produce may be of the greatest value, he intends only his own gain, and he is in this, as in many other cases, led by an invisible hand to promote an end which was no part of his intention.

Here, again, the promises of the Pied Pipers—government planners—are *absolutely* impossible of fulfillment. Their coercive input is composed exclusively of errors. If this point were more generally understood, that understanding would put an end to the Command Society. For such understanding, recognize two facts:

1. The productive input for any given year has its origin in literally trillions of ideas, inventions—think-of-thats—by millions of individuals.
2. In not a single instance does any individual know what the next moment will bring forth in the way of a creative idea. New ideas are not foreseen by the

---

[3]See "The New Confusion About 'Planning'" by F. A. Hayek (The *Morgan Guaranty Survey,* January, 1976).

innovators themselves—thus, *could not possibly be foreseen by self-ordained rulers.* How can a Pied Piper see in you that which you have not seen in yourself!

For example, take a "simple" pencil. One of the countless ingredients is a wetting agent: sulphonated tallow—animal fats chemically reacted with sulphuric acid. Imagine the number of individuals, the span of time, the experimental failures and steps forward in bringing sulphuric acid into existence! And who or how many had a hand in chemically reacting this "oil of vitriol" with animal fats to make possible a "simple" pencil? Simple? The creative process, even in the simplest items, baffles the imagination of anyone who will seriously peer below the surface and, by so doing, realize that here indeed are countless miracles at the human level.

Those who promise much and perform *absolutely* nothing are wicked in the sense that they are motivated by vanity rather than morality. Samuel Butler's explanation:

> Authority intoxicates
> And makes sots of magistrates.
> The fumes of it invade the brain,
> And make men selfish, proud and vain.

False promises intended to advance power over others are clearly immoral. And the same can be said of false promises that are unintentional, those born of ignorance. Falsifying is wicked, regardless of the reason for lying.

Enough of the wicked. What about their opposite, the righteous, the ones who promise little and perform much? Who are they? They are the millions who, year in and year out, have trillions of ideas, seeking their own gain, and who serve all of us with their productive efforts. They are classed by Sumner as forgotten men.

Why forgotten? The knowledge of how freedom works its wonders is so infinitesimal that these unintentional benefactors are not generally recognized as such, which makes it plausible for the Pied Pipers to claim the credit for our welfare.

Forgotten men? They are rarely known to be the source of our well-being in the first place; and further, they do not even think of themselves as such. This explains why they go on playing host to the rapidly growing number of parasites.

A final thought. Take any one of these millions you care to choose, for instance, one of the many who had a hand in a pencil's wetting agent. Did he promise what he was going to invent or discover prior to the moment an idea flashed into mind? Impossible! His performance alone is the extent of his promise.

We have in these productive millions—so far as promises and performances are concerned—the righteous. They are our unintentional benefactors—miracle workers. They are so little recognized that we might call them the secret agents of the free market. One of these days one or more of us will find a way to replace this secrecy with understanding and clarity—a greatly needed performance. Then? *Everyone will win!*

16

THE CASE FOR SEEKING

No one knows more than a millionth of one per cent of anything. —**THOMAS ALVA EDISON**

Edison's phrase, "a millionth of one per cent," is a figure of speech. Had he said a trillionth or an octillionth he would have made his point. Why? Whatever the fraction, Edison's meaning has to do with our *finite* understanding relative to *Infinite* Knowledge, Intelligence, Consciousness. Comparing a particle of dust to a galaxy would suggest only an infinitesimal beginning of this infinite difference—limitless!

Thomas Edison excelled any human being known to me—past or present—in the sheer quantity of what he knew; bits of knowledge by the tens of thousands. But he was really knowledgeable only in contrast with other humans who do not know "more than a millionth of one per cent of anything."

There is, however, a crowning accolade we can confer upon this inventive genius: *he knew so much that he knew he knew nothing!* As Socrates remarked: "I know nothing, but I know I know nothing." This is the brand of knowledge—really the only kind—that can grace humanity.

At the outset, a confession. My aim in life resembles

Edison's in one respect—inventiveness. He aimed at inventing electrical and comparable aids to mankind—the incandescent bulb, for instance. And succeeded beyond the dreams of those who had gone before! My aim for years has encompassed the freedom philosophy and *inventing* ways to communicate the appropriate methods for a restoration of freedom. Up until now I have failed so miserably that I know I don't know anything—which is one blessing! But I haven't given up, and never intend to do so. By seeking, I have come upon a clue that could lead to success, a truism by the wizard of Menlo Park: "No one knows more than a millionth of one per cent of anything." Thanks to you, wonderful wizard!

One of the most brilliant individuals of my wide acquaintance, when asked, "How are you, Hutch?" would respond, "Compared to what?" When compared to the rest of us, he was near the top of the intellectual and philosophical totem pole. But—and this is my point—when compared to Infinite Knowledge, he ranked with Edison, Socrates, Leonardo da Vinci, all the kings, politicians, and bureaucrats who have inhabited this earth—a mere neophyte! Hutch, in this latter ranking, knew nothing; but, bless his soul, he knew it!

Reflect on the manner in which most people grade themselves. The question, "compared to *what*?" never enters their heads. They rarely judge themselves in terms of the highest principles they know; rather, it is "compared to *whom*?"—other people. And what fallacies they tumble into by using this unmindful form of self-assessment! They ferret out other people's shortcomings, and then compare some strength of theirs with the weakness of another. They elevate themselves into a feeling of general superiority if they happen to be merely a better speaker, actor, musician, novelist, manufacturer, politician, power monger, or any other of countless thousands of occupations. They fail to realize that all human beings above the moronic level are superior to them in one or more ways. Without question, all of us are neophytes, more particularly those who don't know they know not—the big I-AMS!

It is necessary to compare our finite minds with the Infinite Mind in order to recognize what neophytes we are. Indeed, there is no human being—past or present—who has the slightest idea of his own composition. Composed, as I am, of 1,000,000,000,000,000,000,000,000,000 atoms, I don't even know what an atom is. Nor does anyone else!

Considering that I know not one octillionth of one per cent of anything—a lowly neophyte, indeed—reflect on the utter absurdity of my coercively running your life. Even God doesn't lord it over us, but millions of neophytes do. Egomania on the rampage!

Exposing the dictocratic absurdity, however, is not the object of this brevity. Rather, I wish to comment critically on what seems to be a common folly on the part of ever so many who recognize the dictocratic absurdity, are alarmed at what's going on, and are determined to correct the mess we're in. 'Tis their method that is here at issue; they're bent on reforming teachers, students, employees, clergymen, businessmen, labor union officials, neighbors—everyone who doesn't stand against the rapidly growing socialism.

What's the pitch of one so cocksure of himself? "Beam my ideas at them" or "I must *reach* this or that category of the population," is the gist of this rapidly growing tactic.

It's nothing less than "If those nincompoops were only up to me in their thinking, all would be hunky-dory." Were all like me, think what a wonderful world this would be!

But such a thought is instantly absurd once I realize what a lowly neophyte I am. Multiply a zero times ten, a million, or an octillion, and the answer is still zero.

How do we move away from this zero position, this nothingness? The formula which I have repeated time and again is simple: Instead of trying to reach others, see if we can achieve that point in understanding—attractiveness—when others will reach for us. Away with trying to cast others in our images. First, it can't be done; second, nothing would be gained were it possible.

The answer is in *seeking*, not human duplicates, but truth. Seemingly, most of those in today's world have all but forgotten what a few of the ancients so clearly perceived:

> Ask, and it shall be given you; seek, and ye shall find; knock, and it shall be opened unto you. For everyone that asketh receiveth; and he that seeketh findeth; and to him that knocketh it shall be opened.   *Matthew VII:7-8*

For those of us interested in human freedom—each individual free to act creatively as he or she pleases—let the method fit the problem: *seeking*. Believing this, I sought and came upon that enlightening truism by Thomas Alva Edison quoted at the head of this chapter. Edison's humility before Truth is a revelation by *one* who knew that he didn't know one millionth of one per cent of anything. I'll wager that he did a lot of knocking, for observe all that opened unto him. May all freedom devotees learn from this man, remarkable compared to *whom*? To the most of us—by far!

17

AM I A PART
OF THE PROBLEM?

If you are not a part of the solution, you are a part of the problem. **—UNKNOWN**

Are you a part of the social problem, contributing to the present mess we're in? The answer is yes—unless you are a part of the solution! However, and in spite of inclinations to the contrary, it is not my role to answer that question for you or anyone else but, rather, to assess my own status in the scheme. If, perchance, this analysis of self helps another shift from being a part of the problem to becoming a part of the solution, then that's reward enough for me.

Why, in this wise observation by an author unknown to me, is "a part" so much emphasized? Is it not because no individual is more than an infinitesimal element in either the solution or the problem? Each of us is but a drop in the sea of humanity, not just of our time but of all time, and not just in our community or nation but in the whole world. Should I fail to recognize this fact—my limitations—I will attempt to cast others in my image, in which case I *remain a part of the problem*.

The sea of humanity is composed of human drops—you and me and everyone else—no less than the Red Sea or any other body of water is a multiple of water drops. But note this: It is the purity or impurity of the drops, be they human or water, that determine the purity or impurity of the seas. My role is obvious. It is to set my sights and actions aright. If I do, then I will become *a part of the solution!*

In order to set my sights and actions aright, I must first settle on a standard of right and a measure of wrong, that is, on society's ideal and society's nemesis. What are these opposites? *Freedom and slavery!* The latter has numerous contemporary labels: communism, Fabianism, fascism, naziism, and so on. This is to say that to the extent politicians and bureaucrats control our creative activities, and to the degree that our labors are coercively directed to satisfy the desires of others rather than selves, to that extent are we slaves. Bundle these several forms of political slavery under one label: socialism. Here's my definition:

> Socialism is the state ownership and control of the *means* of production (the planned economy) and the state ownership and control of the *results* of production (the welfare state).

Very well! What is the first step I must take in order to shift from being a part of the problem to becoming a part of the solution? Do no wrong, say no wrong, even think no wrong! I must learn never to give any encouragement or lend any support to a single ideological error. Simple? Not exactly!

First, I must not only be able to recite the definition of wrong—socialism—but must also apprehend its full significance in my mind. The truly difficult part is to assess each and every political activity and draw an accurate conclusion as to whether it is right or wrong. If any political action even prepares the ground for socialism, it is wrong and therefore should never be encouraged.

Most people identify socialistic activities as the programs and propaganda currently emanating from the Kremlin—the "communist conspiracy." However, wrap the American flag around any one of these for a short period and it's labeled "Americanism." Once, while making this point in a lecture, I remarked, "Most people do not think of our postal system as a socialistic institution." A listener interrupted with, "Of course it isn't; we've had it so long." Typical!

The first step does not require of me that I be a creative thinker, writer, talker of the freedom philosophy but *only* that I partake in no wrong. Nothing else! But never overlook the importance of those who do no wrong. No longer are they a part of the problem; rather, they are a part of the solution. Rarely recognized is the fact that those who never do wrong have an enormous radiating influence.

"Do no wrong" is the first part of this beginner's level (first-step) exemplarity. The second? It is difficult, if not impossible, to know what's wrong unless one has a reasonably fair awareness of what's right. Is this companion part difficult? Though too seldom taken, not at all! An estimation of what's right is as simple as the ABC's—if I be in my right mind. What is the right mind? One's own! For me it is my mind, not somebody else's. And for you, by the same token, it is your mind, and not mine. Of course, I absorb what I can from those who are in their right minds but it is my mind that decides who are and are not in their right minds.

A startling bit of truth comes to light in this observation, a way of assessing what I am or am not. If what's right or wrong—freedom or slavery—isn't readily identifiable, I am not in my right mind; rather, I am a mere shadow of countless others who are not in their right minds.

I look around my own orbit and observe the many who do no thinking for themselves; they reflect only what they hear and read. Unfortunately, many who have the public ear and eye are no more in their right minds than the ones swayed by their jargon. These influence peddlers, by and large, are but articulate broadcasters of socialism: *slavery!*

To repeat, becoming a part of the solution rather than a part of the problem requires as a first step *only* that I do no wrong. Elbert Hubbard, who clearly perceived the distinction between freedom and slavery—a man in his right mind—bequeathed to posterity—you and me—a mode of behavior that anyone in his right mind can easily grasp and practice:

I wish to be simple, honest, natural, frank, clean in mind and clean in body, unaffected—ready to say "I do not know," if so be it— . . . to face any obstacles and meet every difficulty unafraid and unabashed. I wish to live without hate, whim, jealousy, envy or fear. I wish others to live their lives, too—up to their highest, fullest and best. To that end I pray that I may *never meddle, dictate, interfere, give advice that is not wanted,* nor assist when my services are not needed. If I can help people, I will do it by giving them a chance to help themselves; and if I can uplift or inspire, let it be by example, inference and suggestion, *rather than by injunction and dictation.* I desire to Radiate Life. (Italics mine)

Radiate Life! Those who do no wrong have an enormous radiating influence.

True, there are higher steps: (1) becoming creative thinkers and expositors of the freedom philosophy and (2) rising to such a high state of excellence that others will seek our tutorship. These advanced steps are never to be expected until the first step is taken. The first step opens the portals to one's potentialities. Doing no wrong casts a light on the undiscovered self; it is the preface to the expansion of consciousness. But even if these higher blessings never come to pass, doing no wrong assures an escape from being a part of the problem and rising to a part of the solution. It is the way to Radiate Life!

18

WHERE LOOK FOR
OUR EMANCIPATORS?

*In every epoch of the world, the
great event. . . . is it not the arrival
of a thinker?*—**THOMAS CARLYLE**

The greatest epoch in all history, in my estimation, was 2,000 years ago. The next greatest epoch—a flowering of the first—graced this land of ours 200 years ago. However, there is a third in the offing, barely visible but in sight, which may be of even greater importance to Americans than the second.

The second, heralded by the Declaration of Independence, was an example of action and reaction. The action? Old-world tyranny! The reaction? Freedom in a new world on a scale never before experienced!

So what is the action that features the third? A plunge into all-out socialism—not over there but *right here!* The required reaction? A rebirth of freedom in this once land of the free!

At the outset, I differ with one point in Carlyle's observation. True, "the great event" in earlier history was brought about by "the arrival of *a* thinker." But the Declaration of Independence was brought about not by one but by several thinkers. And several thinkers, not *a* thinker will, in my humble opinion, bring about the third epoch—the one in the offing. Is this not the way it should be? Is it not the fulfillment of the Second Coming? To me, at least, this does not mean the Coming of another Christ—the Perfect Exemplar—but, rather, the coming, as nearly as possible, of such exemplarity in each individual.

My thesis is that we are to look for our emancipators among the active thinkers. How many are required, and in what walks of life will they be found? Suppose this question had been raised a few years prior to the signing of the Declaration. No one could have answered. Of this we can be certain: only an infinitesimal fraction of the population—signers and others—had at once the wisdom and the courage to bring such a document as the Declaration into existence.

From what walks of life did the signers come? Who could have guessed? Two were physicians, another the son of a clergyman. Included were a lawyer, a merchant, an importer, a musician, a printer, a carpenter, a cobbler, a cooper, and even a millionaire.

I am convinced that the number—"the several thinkers"—who will be responsible for switching our nation from socialism to freedom will, percentage-wise, be no greater than it was 200 years ago—again an infinitesimal fraction. Does not the U.S.A. have more than a tiny fraction of such thinkers today? No, not of the required quality! The best freedom devotees among us have only scratched the surface when it comes to making the case for the free society. Neither I—nor anyone else—can achieve the required understanding short of acknowledging that we all have more—much more—to learn. Why should not each of us accept this seemingly harsh judgment by Simon Ben Azzai? "In seeking wisdom thou art wise; in imagining that thou hast attained it, thou art a fool."

There are politicians and bureaucrats by the millions who imagine that they have attained wisdom—a foolish notion—or they would not believe that they are more capable of running your life and mine better than we can. This is the darkness which engulfs present-day America. However, it is easily demonstrable that darkness has not the slightest resistance to light and, by the same token, ignorance—foolishness—has no resistance to the seeking of wisdom: enlightenment! Thus, the solution rests with seekers of wisdom, thinkers of extraordinary caliber.

From what walks of life will such thinkers come? Again, who knows! The other day I received a letter from a ten-year-old lad who showed a better grasp of the free market philosophy than is presently evidenced by most Ph.D's!

To understand the nature of our problem, consider the severe and relentless attacks upon business from every conceivable source, including some businessmen themselves. On the other hand, many businessmen around the nation are frantically attempting to defend business enterprise against these ruthless blows. Are we to expect thinkers of the required quality to emerge from among these distraught persons? Yes, one now and then; but expect no more real thinkers from the ranks of businessmen than from other walks of life—physicians, clergymen, importers, printers, carpenters, cobblers, or whatever profession. No more now than was the case 200 years ago.

A fact rarely suspected, let alone understood, is that businessmen are by no means the chief beneficiaries of the free market, private ownership, limited government way of life. Many business ventures fail entirely. Who then are the beneficiaries? *The masses!*

Politicians, bureaucrats, editors, news commentators, "economists," "teachers," and other word artists who denounce private enterprise and praise socialism are their own worst enemies. By attacking and maligning those who try to out-compete others in order to make as much of a fortune as possible, these attackers are *unwittingly* destroying the sources of their own livelihood. They kill the geese that lay the golden eggs—and don't know it!

Nor do businessmen, except in rare instances, have the welfare of the masses at heart. They labor to make money but in doing so they *unwittingly* serve others!

Here we have one of the explanations for the mess we're in. When those served know not who their benefactors are, and when those who serve are unaware of the ones whom they serve, we have a know-nothing society—dying on the vine, as we say.

How to be done with this know-nothingness, this *unwitting* nonsense? From whom the required enlightenment? From a thinker, one who can replace the nonsense with sense! Where look for such a person? The one seen in the mirror but who, if like me, must look around for help. My help came from a Yale professor, the late William Graham Sumner. Let only a few absorb the full meaning of these simple sentences and ours will be a growing, not a dying-on-the-vine society:

> Every man and woman in society has one big duty. That is, *to take care of his or her own self.* This is a *social* duty. For, fortunately, the matter stands so that the duty of making the best of one's self is not a separate thing from the duty of filling one's place in society, but the *two are one, and the latter is accomplished when the former is done.*[1] (Italics mine)

Being one of the masses—not a businessman—and sharing Sumner's enlightenment, what practices of businessmen do I disapprove or approve? I disapprove of the growing number who "think" that they have a "social responsibility"—looking out for the likes of me. This notion is no less repulsive than that of the political know-it-alls, the ones who foolishly imagine that they can run your life and mine better than we can. Those in either group—one as much as the other—imagine that they have attained wisdom. An interesting aside: the bureaucrats finance their egomania with taxpayer's money, and these equally foolish businessmen finance their egomania with stockholder's money! So I ask, with Montaigne: "What more wretched than the man who is the slave of his own imaginings?"

The businessmen I approve? Astonishingly, the ones who are doing their level best to make money! Bless their economic souls! They are my material benefactors, even though they may not have the slightest idea that they are performing such a role. They are taking care of their own selves, and so long as their dealings are open and above

---

[1]*What Social Classes Owe to Each Other*, p. 98.

board—honest—that's their main social duty, and their sole duty to me and others of the masses.

Of the ones I approve, who are the highest in my esteem? Those who are the most successful, who get way out ahead of all competitors, the further ahead the better; those who make their fortunes in the market place.

Why this unorthodox way of looking at our economic world? The answer is simple: others like to get out ahead, as in a horse race; they like to make money too. As a consequence, countless others will try to outperform the leading performers. Many will fail, of course. But examine any endeavor in the business world and we find that someone always comes up with a better idea and leapfrogs the one out front. And what does the better idea turn out to be? Some good or service that we of the masses prefer above other available resources. The free market, private ownership, limited government way of life is a game of leapfrog; and all of us, even the avowed socialists, prosper from this little-understood game of serving consumers. And many of those successful businessmen don't even know what wonderful service they render!

From the foregoing comments, one may wonder why my insistence that our emancipators must be composed of more advanced thinkers than have heretofore graced our society? Suppose there were to emerge among us thinkers on a par with our Founding Fathers. Would not that quality suffice? No, for their problem was in no way comparable to our present dilemma.

Our Founding Fathers, fed up with Old-World tyranny, sought freedom. The essence of their ambition? I wish to be my own man rather than some tyrant's man! And their thinking was of that high quality which brought fulfillment. However, these ancestors of ours did not—could not— foresee the miracles that would be wrought when, for the first time in history, there was little if any organized force standing against the release of creative human energy. They had no precedent to go by, nor were they oracular. "Oracles, like dreams, can only be judged after the event."

After the event? After the greatest outburst of creativity ever known to mankind. In all respect for their wisdom, our Founding Fathers did not know that this would be one of freedom's dividends. And even after the event, few indeed are those who begin to see clearly what happened and why. Merely take note of the followers of this or that ideology who take credit for the American miracle. Today's tyrants—those who think they can run your life and mine better than we can—resemble the tyrants of old in proclaiming themselves the authors of the American miracle. And they declare freedom to be the enemy of human progress. The opposite of truth is on the rampage.

The problem? I repeat, not a person known to me has more than scratched the surface when it comes to making the case for the free market. The ideological cards are stacked against us. The solution? Let each one of us try his best; and among the thousands who try, several will gain that enlightenment against which tyranny cannot endure. These several, and these alone, will be our emancipators. May you, whoever you are, become an emancipator. Let's play our own free market game of leapfrogging one another in our understanding and practice of freedom.

19

LET'S LOOK TO
OUR PRINCIPLES

*If it's right in principle, it has to
work!* —**BENJAMIN A. ROGGE**

The reference here is not only to material progress for self
and others, but also to intellectual and moral progress—
emergence—of individuals. These aspects of progress are
interrelated and inseparable. We want things to work, for
nearly everyone prefers progress to decadence. Our desire
is that we rise to a superior way of life, rather than fall into
one that is inferior. The question is, how can one tell
whether or not he is on the right course? Rogge gives the
answer: "If it's right in principle, it has to work!"

This answer, while unquestionably correct, is far easier to
state than its guideline is to interpret. "Right in principle"
can be compared to truth in its pristine purity. No one in his
right mind claims to possess this. Our fallible minds can
purge a theory of some errors; but all? What then do we
have to go by? Pragmatic considerations mainly; does it or
does it not work! If affirmative, we have hit upon a right

principle; if negative, a wrong principle. But the question *does it work?* has about as many diverse answers as there are persons who raise the question. A few samples:

- The thief "thinks" *robbery* is a right principle—taking great risks for the sake of small and momentary gains. In his ignorant estimation, it works.
- The politicians and bureaucrats who utter only those words which will get votes or popular approval believe *expediency* is a right principle because "it works," that is, it puts or keeps them in office.
- Labor union officials who use force to obtain above-market wages and below-market hours for their members believe *coercion* to be a right principle. To them, it seems to work.
- Businessmen who persuade government to impose tariffs and other restrictions to free and uninhibited trade, believe *monopoly* to be a right principle. Being nearsighted, they "think" it works.
- Teachers who advance spend-ourselves-rich notions, "think" *Keynesism* to be a right principle. With their limited vision, they do not understand why it does not work.
- Clergymen who preach that brand of welfarism which consists of robbing Peter to pay Paul believe, no less than thieves, that *robbery* is a right principle. To these shortsighted "religionists," it gives the appearance of working.

It takes but a slight amount of insight and foresight to recognize that not one of the above "works." Each of them brings destruction, as becomes obvious upon reflection.

Suppose all were thieves—all parasites and no hosts.

Everyone would perish. *Robbery* violates the right to the fruits of one's own labor and, thus, is wrong in principle.

Suppose all were word mongers—everyone telling lies. Why would all perish? Lying violates truth; *expediency* is wrong in principle.

Suppose every citizen were a coercionist—freedom to act creatively completely squelched. None would survive. *Coercion* restrains creativity and is wrong in principle.

Suppose all were monopolists—every good and service having but a single human source, not an iota of competition or exchange of ideas, inventions, discoveries. No survivors! *Monopoly* restrains the freedom to produce and exchange, and is wrong in principle.

Suppose all were Keynesians. Society would revert to primitive barter, and nearly all would perish. *Keynesism* causes inflation and destroys an honest, workable medium of exchange; it is wrong in principle.

Obviously, all of the above are restraints; not a one will work, for they are founded on a wrong principle. To repeat, "If it's right in principle, it has to work." What then is right in principle? My answer: Discover what should be *released* and what *restrained*. It is right in principle, then, to restrain every action which hinders the release of creative energy. And, by the same token, it is right in principle to release every action which facilitates creative energy.

How does creative human energy manifest itself? Overly simplified, in an overall luminosity, that unimaginable wisdom which emerges—blossoms—as a social phenomenon when the creativity of all individuals is released and *free to flow*. The term I have used—"wisdom of the market"—is too mundane for communicating what I mean. Frankly, this social phenomenon is nothing less than Creation manifesting itself at the human level. What name shall we give this wisdom which exists in no one person but exclusively in a free flowing of infinitesimal bits of insights, intuitive flashes, and the like? Why not call this indescribable phenomenon *Creativity,* and let it go at that!

It is Creativity that works and it's the only force that does! It has to work because it is right in principle. Restrain not an iota of it; release Creativity 100 per cent—not an exception! Admittedly, this is one of the least understood of all politico-economic truths. Try as one will, over and over again, and it is rarely grasped. It is in the realm of the spiritual and can only be caught, not taught. But this we know: it is in the free market, private ownership, limited government way of life that Creativity flowers to bless mankind.

The best one can do to prove this point is to ask of anyone that he cite a single creative action that should be restrained. Name an exception; that's our unabashed challenge!

Immanuel Kant laid down the rule for the kind of behavior on which the right principle is founded:

Act only on that maxim [principle] which you can at the same time will that it should become a universal law.

This is to say that no one should ever act in a manner contrary to his ideal of how all persons should act toward one another. The instruction is clear: If any action of mine would result in social chaos if practiced by everyone, then I must never so act. Let everyone measure his own conduct by the yardstick he applies to others. In essence, the Golden Rule—exemplarity!

Henry Ward Beecher contributed an enlightening thought to this theme: "Expedients are for the hour, principles for the ages."

In the economic realm, Henry Hazlitt adds his Creativity:

Economics . . . is the science of tracing the effects of some proposal or existing policy not only on some special interest in the short run but on the *general interest in the long run.*

If right principle is to guide our thoughts and actions, only those proposals or existing policies merit approval which could be lived with forever. There is no such thing as a short-range gain that is not also a blessing in the long run—forever! To assess any action as a gain for the hour that is not a gain for the ages is nothing but faulty assessment, an inability to see beyond one's nose, as the saying goes. It is to miss the whole point of Creativity at the human level.

If it's right in principle, it has to work; therefore, let's look to our principles.

20

THE CHARITABLE ECONOMIST

With malice toward none; with charity for all.
—ABRAHAM LINCOLN

Of formal schooling, it can be accurately said of poverty-stricken Abe that he had almost none. However, so avid was he for learning that he schooled himself. Lincoln is one of a number of noted persons who lacked schooling, but educated himself; and, self-education is, in a very real sense, the only education there is. Not compulsory "learning," not the craving for degrees or fame or position but, rather, the avidity for learning is, quite obviously, the key to growth in understanding. How many high-titled "economists" in today's world could originate such a profound thought as "With malice toward none; with charity for all"? Not many! But to be charitable, I must never accuse them of not knowing what such wisdom is all about!

Is charity a lost virtue? Surface appearances—all we can see—suggest its rarity. Depersonalized philanthropy may be commendable, but it is not charity. During recent decades, and on an enormous scale, millions of people simply write checks to institutions, and these agencies serve as committees to decide who the beneficiaries are to be. By this type of escapism, the relationship between giver and receiver becomes nonexistent, and "The gift without the giver" is no more charity than throwing checks to the four winds. Call it an idle response to "Let organizations assume our godliness," but never put this in the category of charity.

True charity is exclusively in the realm of the hidden. I cannot see it in you but, even more significant, you cannot see it in yourself. The true kind? Here is my authority:[1]

> Thus, when you do some act of charity, do not announce it with a flourish of trumpets, as the hypocrites do in synagogue and in the streets to win admiration from men. I tell you this: they have their reward already. No; when you do some act of charity, *do not let your left hand know what your right is doing; your good deed must be a secret.*

There are those who know that when one casts his bread—kindly deeds, charities—upon the waters—fellowmen—that the returns are many fold. Yet, should returns be the motivation, the loaves will not multiply but vanish. True charity is a spiritual attainment, a harmonizing with Infinite Consciousness. The left hand does not, must not, know what the right is doing. This comes close, I believe, to what was in Lincoln's mind when he wrote, "with charity for all."

Now then, what did this President of the U.S.A. mean in his Second Inaugural Address (March 4, 1865) by the phrase

---

[1]Matthew V:6.

"With malice toward none?" He repudiated "active ill will; desire to harm others, or do mischief; spite." At this point, it is appropriate to ask, how did I ever come upon such an unusual accolade as "The charitable economist?" By reading Honest Abe, one who schooled himself. Reflect on these two examples of his wisdom:

> My faith in the proposition that each man should do precisely as he pleases with all which is exclusively his own, lies at the foundation of the sense of justice there is in me. I extend the principle to communities of men, as well as to individuals. I extend it, because it is politically wise, as well as naturally just: politically wise, in saving us from broils about matters which do not concern us.[2]
>
> Property is the fruit of labor. Property is desirable, is a positive good in the world. That some should be rich shows that others may become rich and hence is just encouragement to industry and enterprise. *Let not him who is houseless pull down the house of another,* but let him work diligently to build one for himself, thus by example assuring that his own shall be safe from violence. . . . I take it that it is best for all to leave each man free to acquire property as fast as he can. Some will get wealthy. *I don't believe in a law to prevent a man from getting rich; it would do more harm than good.*[3]

What a splendid figure of speech: let *not* him who is houseless pull down the house of another! Were I to pull down your house by reason of being houseless myself, as a

---

[2]From *The Collected Works of Abraham Lincoln,* Roy P. Basler, (New Brunswick, N.J., Rutgers University Press, 1953), Vol. II, p. 250.
[3]*Ibid.,* Vol. VII, pp. 259-60.

means of *leveling* your plight and mine, that assuredly would be "active ill will, a desire to harm others." How, pray tell, describe this other than as *malice?*

However, coercive leveling is a form of malice no matter how achieved. When one personally and openly pulls down another's house—destroys property—the crime is readily apparent; anyone graced with common sense regards the act as a rank injustice, as malice. But depersonalize the act by getting government—organized coercive force—to commit the identical crime, and shame disappears. Recognized malice is converted into a naive innocence. A sense of absolution replaces all feeling of wrongdoing. Tragic, but true!

Reflect on the millions of people in today's America who feather their own nests at the expense of others and, pitifully, think nothing of it! The leveling schemes in our hundred thousand governments have never been counted—they are too numerous. The 16,000,000 on food stamps? They are but a drop in the leveling bucket!

On the present scale, these schemes can be financed only by inflation—a *dilution* of the medium of exchange. Whoever you are, merely observe how your house is being pulled down, your money diminishing in value, the trend accelerating. Who can estimate the number of citizens who have worked and saved and put aside an adequate nest egg for old age or retirement—only to see it eroded by inflation. And, by reasons of this, they too are running to the government trough. All because of naive malice!

Honest Abe, a charitable economist, did not believe in laws that prevent citizens from getting rich; such laws do more harm than good. The U.S.A.'s progressive income tax (plank #2 in the *Communist Manifesto*) is but one of countless laws that are undeniably doing more harm than good, particularly to the poor. And all of them—no exception—are economic weeds seeded by naive malice!

Malice, an example of human error, cannot be downed until it is found and understood. And when discovered and uncovered, there lies truth: *Charity for all.*

Becoming a charitable economist is an attainment possible for any alert individual. Give America a fair number and there will be a renewed and Holy ring to:

Our father's God, to Thee
Author of Liberty.

21

THE GOOD LIFE: A FLOWING ACTION

The truest view of life has always seemed to me to be that which shows that we are here not to enjoy, but to learn.
—**F. W. ROBERTSON**

As I see it, the truest view of life is that we are here to learn *and* to enjoy. While learning, if it be truly such, is enjoyable in all walks of life, my reference in what follows will be to learning about freedom—the good life.

By "enjoy" I do not have in mind the frivolous kind such as entertainment and the like or, as the dictionary has it: "not properly serious or sensible; silly and light-minded; giddy." Learning and enjoying, properly understood, belong together. My belief: *Learning, if it be "truly such," is unquestionably life's most enjoyable experience*. I agree with Aristotle: "To learn gives the liveliest pleasure, not only to philosophers but to men in general." This is a conviction greatly in need of explanation if freedom is to prevail, for self if not for others.

125

But first, a few thoughts as to the kind of learning that is "truly such," the kind that should, in my view, be one's ambition. Believing that all actions, even the most serious, should be joyous—fun—here's support for the idea in the humor of Will Rogers: "So live life that you wouldn't be ashamed to sell the family parrot to the town gossip." The instruction? The seeking of righteousness is first and foremost in the kind of learning that is "truly such"—approval from God, not by the gossipy ilk. Merely to stuff one's mind with the currently fashionable information and slogans of most public media is not learning; it gives us no useful ideas on which to base constructive and creative human action.

One way to draw the distinction between the two kinds of learning is to recognize that it is easy to learn something about many things, but absolutely impossible to learn everything about anything. The more we learn about any one thing—be it an atom, a snowflake or galaxy—the more we know we don't know—the greater the mystery. Increasing mystery identifies the kind of learning that is "truly such," the kind that is life's most enjoyable experience. The other, the popular kind that bedevils our society, was lampooned in *Poor Richard's Almanac:* "A learned blockhead is a greater blockhead than an ignorant one."

One needs, however, more explanations of the type of learning we are here for, the learning that relates to freedom—the good life. That it is a flowing action should be self-evident, flowing since the dawn of language. As Henry Hazlitt suggests, we could accomplish nothing if we had to depend on our own unaided efforts. We could not think above the level of a chimpanzee if we did not inherit the priceless gift of an already-created language. We think in words, an inheritance that is obviously a *flowing* action.

Learning, the kind worthy of praise, is also a *growing* action. A brilliant observation: "One does not grow old; one becomes old by not growing." Growing in what dimension? In awareness, perception, consciousness; in a word, Becoming! That's what we are here for: emergence—no arrest at any level of learning—by self or by political or any other kind of know-it-alls. When on the right course—emerging which freedom permits—flowing and growing are related actions and occur simultaneously. This, unquestionably, is life's most enjoyable experience.

True learning is the seeking of truth now and always. Karl Jaspers phrased it thus:

The Greek word for philosopher (*philosophos*) . . . signifies the lover of wisdom (knowledge) as distinguished from him who considers himself wise in the possession of knowledge. The meaning of the word still endures: the essence of philosophy is not the possession of truth but the search for truth, regardless of how many philosophers may belie it with their dogmatism, that is, with a body of didactic principles purporting to be definitive and complete. Philosophy means *to be on the way*. Its questions are more essential than its answers, and every answer becomes a new question.

And Stewart Edward White reports a revelation as to how we should respect truth as each of us understands it:

One acquires a truth as one believes in it, and admits it, and tries to stick to it. Until that truth has become to you an unfailing motive power; until you cannot help acting any way but in it; until you are one of its supporting elements, as it were, you do not gain the full benefit of its possession.

There are those among us who regard the free market, private ownership, limited government way of life—freedom of the individual to act creatively as he pleases—as a truth so nearly approximating Divine Intention that we admit it and try to stick to it. We seek to be one of its supporting elements.

We are, however, faced with not less than three obstacles which must be understood or they will overrun and the truth as we see it will not prevail:

1. Despair: Manifested by millions of dictocrats who would run our lives, plus the millions who blindly follow them.
2. Apathy: Our belief cannot be a possession of society or even of ourselves until we can demonstrate its workability.
3. Uniqueness: The flowing, growing action—the very essence of the good life—is accompanied by many dropouts or changeovers which, if the reasons be not known, can lead to a discouragement so pronounced that some workers in freedom's vineyard will become dropouts themselves.

The first obstacle is an erroneous assessment, namely that freedom has no chance short of mass—majority— understanding and approval. Straighten out the millions! Any individual who entertains this false notion must conclude that our case is hopeless. He throws in the sponge— one less worker in freedom's vineyard—a dropout!

Have a look at history to remedy this mood of despair. All turnabouts from the bad to the good life have been led by an infinitesimal minority. The most important movement in Western Civilization was achieved by a Leader and a dozen Disciples. Jefferson and two or three others wrote freedom's greatest political document: The Declaration of Independence. Two men—Richard Cobden and John Bright—turned England around following the Napoleonic wars. Three men—Ludwig von Mises, Wilhelm Roepke and Ludwig Erhard—performed a similar miracle in devastated West Germany shortly after World War II. Saviors are always few in number.[1]

The second obstacle, namely, the notion that freedom cannot grace society or even ourselves unless we can explain its workability, is a profound challenge. It can be met only by a growing action by free men. Many of us know that freedom does work wonders but not one, to my knowledge, has explained with sufficient clarity *why* its workability. Our explanations are in need of continuing refinement. What to do? Love the challenge—the formula for perpetual improvement!

Now to the third obstacle. To avoid discouragement, we must speculate on why the dropouts and changeovers are so numerous. Over the past 43 years I have watched them come and go by the thousands: from neophytes to devotees to goners—from seekers to jumping-up-and-down enthusiasts to memories. Should this not depress you and me? Not at all if the reasons be known. Here are three of them:

---

[1]For an explanation of the last two assertions, see the chapters, "The Point of Cure" and "Right Now!" in my *The Love of Liberty*, FEE, 1975.

1. In more than four decades many have gone to their reward.
2. Others have grown above your and my offerings— graced by intellectual and moral ascension. Unless we have ascended far enough ourselves, we know not of their existence. Reflect on those in today's world who have never heard of Mises, for instance.
3. The good life is a flowing action and, as a consequence, many have discovered a uniqueness they prefer to the study and exposition of how freedom works its wonders. They become contributors to the material welfare of all. Why look upon this as a gain rather than a loss? All would perish were mankind dependent on the production of goods and services by the very few leaders responsible for the turnabouts toward freedom—the good life!

A final question: If one recognizes the value and importance of freedom, how can he best make use of such freedom and contribute to its maintenance and support?

Above all else, recognize that we are here to learn *and* to enjoy. Learning is most enjoyable when the individual discovers his uniqueness and ardently develops it.

As one sage observed, "Your outgo must equal your intake." In other words, your further reception of good ideas depends upon your sharing the ideas that come to you with those who care to listen. The more one shares his good ideas, the more he learns. Experience attests to this. Advancement of the good life—freedom of the individual to act creatively as he pleases—is founded on sharing—a flowing action.

Why do I share these ideas? In order to enjoy and to help expand my freedom and yours.

22

THE WONDER OF WONDERS

*The world will never starve for the
want of wonders, but only for want
of wonder.* —G. K. CHESTERTON

What did this brilliant Englishman mean by "starve?" The
answer, I believe, is to be found in the words of an earlier
countryman of his, Robert Browning:

> Which lacks food the more,
> Body or soul in me?
> I *starve* in soul.

And "soul?" Again Browning: "God is soul, souls I and
thou!" Translated into modern American idiom it reads,
according to my dictionary, ". . . though having no physical
reality, [soul] is credited with the functions of thinking and
willing, *and hence determines all behavior.*" This is to say
that you and I will think and will our way through life
according to the vitality of our respective souls; our behavior will reflect the health—or sickness—of the life
within. What I wish to examine is the part that wonder plays
in the evolution of the soul, and its vigor.

The way to bring this matter home is to reflect on how we behave when government pre-empts any activity, be it mail delivery, the aid to those in distress, or whatever. We cease to wonder how mail would be delivered were it not socialized, that is, left to the free and unfettered market. Likewise, with the alleviation of distress. Government has pre-empted that; we pay no heed and no longer wonder how Judeo-Christian charity works its wonders. We fall asleep in these and countless other governmental take-overs. Pre-emption of any activity is, except in the case of a few rare souls, the death of wonder!

When government pre-empts any activity or problem area, it thereby closes off that sector against further inquiry or entrepreneurial action—closes the market that otherwise would sift and sort and put to best use the infinite bits and pieces of knowledge in society.

Pre-emption by coercive take-overs accounts for no more than an infinitesimal fraction of the want of wonder. True, we cheer glamorous spectacles as observed in the first of the following verses but the lack of wonder is dramatically illustrated in the second verse:

Fueled by a million man-made wings of fire,
The rocket tore through the sky . . .
And everybody cheered.

Fueled only by a thought from God,
The seedling urged its way through the thickness of black.
And as it pierced the heavy ceiling of the soil
And launched itself up into outer space . . .
No one even clapped.

That seedling is but one of octillions times octillions—indeed, an infinity—of wonders in the Universe. Why, that seedling itself has wonders not remotely comprehended by man. The lack of wonder about Creation—Nature's mysteries—is appalling.

And no less appalling is the lack of wonder about what goes on among those of us who inhabit this earth. Let an electric light bulb come into existence and shortly it is commonplace, taken for granted. No longer any wonder about this fantastic phenomenon or the uniqueness of Edison. Wonder tends to die with familiarity!

Awakened during the night by a jet plane flying over my home, I wondered what would have been my reaction had I lived in Athens at the time of Socrates. Probably, "Good Lord, are the Heavens falling in!" A correct reaction, for that's precisely what's happening. Harken unto this: that jet plane has thousands upon thousands of parts and not a person who lives knows how to make a single one of them—any more than anyone knows how to make a pencil! And a jet plane resembles that seedling in that it is but an infinitesimal fraction of the goods and services by which we presently live and prosper. There is no lack of wonders, only a dearth of wonder.

Let there be no want of wonder about all things in Creation. Wonder in itself is an acknowledgment of one's finite status, the pleasant remedy for disastrous know-it-all-ness and stagnation. Wonder inspires the will to grow and, thus, adds vigor to the soul. Wonder and the spirit of inquiry go hand-in-hand. It is the fountainhead of entrepreneurial action—creativity at the human level. The power of wonder is sublime!

23

THE AUTHENTIC HERO

The hero's will is not that of his ancestors nor of his society, but his own. This will to be oneself is heroism. —ORTEGA

History presents us with countless warrior heroes: Alexander the Great, the several Caesars, Charlemagne, Napoleon, Hitler, Mussolini, on and on to the present day. Such "heroism" is rooted in brute force. And there are even more "heroes" by reason of fame, fortune, notoriety.

Interestingly, the exalted stature of such persons depends upon a boundless hero-worship by the masses. This is to say that the worshipers of these false gods are no less faulty than the self-styled gods who, when worshiped, worship themselves! What a perverse form of worship this is! As one sage observed, "Men are strangely inclined to worship what they do not understand."

Ortega insisted that the hero's will is not that of society—which the above assuredly is. What then is authentic heroism? *The will to be oneself!* Nor is our Spanish philosopher alone in this view:

134

- Emerson: Self-trust is the essence of heroism.
- Beecher: More heroism has been displayed in the household and the closet, than on the most memorable battlefields of history.
- Amiel: Heroism is the brilliant triumph of the soul over the flesh.
- Spencer: Hero worship is strongest where there is the least regard for human freedom.

Emerson's "self-trust" is evidenced by those who abide by their highest conscience. Seek truth from any and all sources and then never deviate from what is believed to be righteous. This is the will to be one's own man, not everybody else's—the will to be one's self! What is heroic about such a demeanor? It takes an enormous amount of intellectual, moral, and spiritual fortitude—the opposite of brute force—to stand ramrod straight, as we say.

Beecher's observation comes through to me as an ingenious aphorism. By "household and closet" he meant one's inner sanctum—the mind. This is the place where real heroism is displayed, in contrast with the unreal heroism of the battlefield variety.

Amiel's "triumph of the soul over the flesh" refers to the priority of righteousness over any pursuit of wealth or power. This is merely another way of phrasing that wonderful Biblical injunction: "Seek ye first the Kingdom of God and His Righteousness, and *these things* shall be added unto you." Briefly, wealth flows as a dividend of authentic heroism. Reverse the admonition by first seeking wealth and there will be neither truth nor wealth. Morality is the wellspring of material things. It cannot be otherwise.

And, finally, the most important of all is Herbert Spencer's truism: "Hero worship is strongest where there is the least regard for human liberty." This is to say that the will to be oneself is weakest where and when liberty does not prevail.

Reflect on the U.S.S.R. or Red China where there is very little regard for human freedom. Hero worship is rampant, the masses kowtowing to the dictocrats. The will to be oneself? That takes courage. Fortunately, history reveals that there is an individual now and then who, regardless of how flagrant the dictatorship, has the will to be himself—Solzhenitsyn, for instance. Were it not for these rare souls who appear unpredictably, there would be no civilized society on this planet—only hero worshipers and the "heroes" worshiping themselves. In the absence of human freedom, there are few emerging, evolving human beings—humanity stagnated!

When government is limited to keeping the peace and invoking a common justice, human freedom prevails. Each individual is on his own; he is free to choose not only what he does but what he thinks or says or writes and, consequently, is self-responsible. A self-responsible person tends to be self-reliant for the simple reason that it is in his self-interest so to be.

It is seldom recognized that freedom is a magnetic force, exerting an attracting power on whatever potentialities there are, to bring them to realization. Freedom draws countless individuals to heights where men have never been before. Freedom spawns authentic heroes who, at the human level, are responsible for such material, intellectual, moral, and spiritual evolution as mankind experiences—the earthly origin of *all* progress!

All of us should do our level best to grasp several points that relate to progress:

- The enormous stake we have in human freedom.
- The rapid replacement of freedom by authoritarianism, that is, by the planned economy and the welfare state: socialism.
- The right diagnosis, so we may know where lies the fault and apply the corrective.

It is my conviction that Goethe correctly pointed to the fault:

None are more hopelessly enslaved than those who falsely believe they are free.

A vast majority of our countrymen today, if asked, "Are you a free man?" would respond, "Of course!" The extent of their enslavement doesn't even dawn upon them.

We hear it said that Americans by the millions are deserting human freedom. This presupposes that they once understood and abided by its principles. People cannot desert that which they never possessed. And the millions, by and large, never had nor do they now have the slightest idea of what human freedom is all about. The citizenry were informed when our country was founded that they were free men and they relied on what they were told. Today? The dictocrats are telling them precisely the same thing and they believe the present-day jargon no less than most of our ancestors accepted the original truth. The masses of our day falsely believe that they are free men. So long as this naivete prevails, they are, as Goethe points out, "hopelessly enslaved."

The fault mainfested all about us, by people in all walks of life—day laborers, businessmen, teachers, clergymen, professional men and women, or whoever—is falsely believing they are free in our present socialistic melee.

What can the correction be? It is personal as one's own conscience and consciousness: the will to be oneself, the birth among us of a few authentic heroes. Thank the Lord that ours is not a numbers problem but, rather, my problem. And, hopefully, you will think of it as yours.

Away with this enslavement, that there may be a return to freedom, the source of progress. Heroism is the answer. Thanks for the enlightenment, Jose Ortega y Gasset!

24

HUMILITY: THE RIGHT ESTIMATE OF SELF

Whoever humbles himself like this
child, is the greatest in the Kingdom
of Heaven.   **MATTHEW XVIII:4**

The largest of all quotation books has nearly 3,000 headings, ranging all the way from *Ability* to *Zeal*. Among the topics is *Humility*—dozens of entries—by this philosopher and that. Other virtues merit numerous entries but *Integrity* does not appear as a heading! This, to me, is an astonishing omission.

Why astonishing? Until now I have always thought of Integrity and Humility as twin virtues, neither possible without the other. But who am I to dispute the great and the wise! They may be right and I wrong. But if so, Integrity must be dismissed as a virtue; it is, perforce, something else. What? But first, here's my understanding of Integrity, a definition I have repeated over and over again:

Integrity is the accurate reflection in word and deed of whatever one's highest conscience dictates as right. This may not in fact be truth but is as close to truth or righteousness as one can get.

If Integrity or Righteousness is not a virtue as is Humility, what then is it? I now believe it is more than a virtue, for without it, all of the virtues—including the first of them, Humility—are out of the question. Expect Humility, Intelligence, Justice, Love, Reverence for Life to flow from those who cannot even be true to themselves let alone to others? From prevaricators, fabricators, dissimulators, liars? Nonsense! Humility can no more be practiced by those not graced with Integrity than by those not graced with a brain. Said the righteous Harry Emerson Fosdick, "Righteousness is first." This is by way of saying that Integrity is the only intellectual and spiritual soil from which Humility can possibly spawn and grow!

Before going further, it is well to emphasize that Integrity does not assure Humility or any of the other virtues. Each must be pondered, reflected upon and, above all, ardently desired or, better yet, prayed for—each a life ambition. Integrity no more than opens the Heavenly gates which, to enter, requires ascension—"the wings of an angel."

The following comments on Humility are not original but, rather my phrasings of observations made by philosophers—seers I hold in high esteem. Included, also, are explanations of what I understand them to mean.

Humility, the right estimate of self, is doubtless the most difficult of all individual achievements. More so than Integrity? Indeed, yes! Integrity is even easier than lying. He who practices Integrity has a single point of reference: that which he believes to be right. He who lies must make accurate references to all the lies he has told. Memory serves no one that well!

Why is Humility so difficult? It takes an enormous

amount of honest, realistic self-scrutiny to grasp just how infinitesimal is one's perception of Infinite Intelligence. Yet, short of this understanding, arrogance captivates the soul, casting the eye downward and not upward, seeing only inferiors and not superiors—beholding fools and not seers. This degrades self and harms others; whereas, Humility, if achieved, uplifts self and helps others.

To dramatize the point, envision in the mind's eye a ladder extending infinitely into space, each of the steps occupied by people possessing varying degrees of perception, from a low level to the highest. All persons on the second step will be superior to those on the first step in at least one respect but, because of individual uniqueness, not in all. How easy for them to become enamored with this next-to-nothing "superiority" and embrace the notion that those on the first step are inferior in every way! Looking down on them! Thus enamored, the eye is not turned to the third step, that is, toward those who have enlightenment to offer for nothing more than the seeking. No growth! Stagnation! Humility, the right estimate of self—knowing that I know not, but wanting to know—is the blessed prescription for an about-face, the sole remedy for a devastating intellectual and moral malady!

"Humble himself like this child." Here we have Humility in its pristine purity. The child sits on no pedestal; looks down on no one; has no exalted opinion of self. The child is fresh from God! What is the most laudable feature of the child? It is his inquisitiveness—wanting to know, looking Heavenward! Nearly seven decades ago, I was a pesky kid, badgering my elders for information. I recall my Uncle John pleading with me, "Leonard, please quit asking so many questions!'' Too bad we can't retain more of this childlikeness as we grow older!

To live in true Humility, to make the most of self, one should never quit this childish trait: looking up, never down—during every moment of mortal life.

Mankind will never perish for wonders; but only for want of wonder. Why? There is an infinitude of wonders. Harmony with the Cosmic Scheme—the evolution of the human spirit, the emergence of perception—requires nothing less than wonder, now and forever. May we, for the good of self and others, emulate the child in pure Humility!

There are ever so many more thoughts in support of Humility, easily found when looking up—seeking from seers. A few brevities:

- One's greatest merit is to know that one's merit is not sufficient.
- How easy to look down on others; no more is required then the ability to stare. But how difficult to look down on one's self! Required? The ability accurately to assess how little one knows!
- It is pride that changes potential seers into those who bedevil themselves; it is only Humility that brings out the best in them.
- Wisdom requires that one not inflate his self-esteem from which a deflationary fall is inevitable. It is wisdom to recognize how lowly is the self, that one may rise.
- It is no problem at all to be humble when brought to a low estate, but to be humble when praised is at once difficult and rare. Remedy? Let praise pass by as a refreshing breeze and be forgotten. Assay criticism for the truth it may contain.

- For Humility to prevail, forgive one's self little if any, but forgive others a great deal.

Wrote Confucius 2,500 years ago: "Humility is the foundation of all the virtues." As I see it now, Integrity forms the foundation, with Humility the greatest potentiality thereof. "To thine own self be true" and pray—forever strive—for the fruit, not only for self but for all others.

25

LET'S COUNT OUR BLESSINGS

My God! how little do my country-men know what precious blessings they are in possession of, and which no other people on earth enjoy. —THOMAS JEFFERSON

Our habits, good and bad, often have strange origins. Rarely can one explain the forces that set up a behavior pattern, nor can I do more than trace the history of a good habit of mine—born in 1964.

We were conducting three successive FEE Seminars at the Mission Inn, Riverside, California. This Saturday was my 66th birthday. Overflowing with gratitude at the way things were going, not only with the Seminars but with me personally, I scribbled on my writing pad 66 blessings—in a few minutes. After finishing, I destroyed the sheet. There was a purpose behind this gesture: Learn to reflect on each day's blessings as sufficient for that day without reference to previous recordings. By following this practice each birthday since 1964, counting my blessings has become a daily habit—and a rewarding one!

144

There's a second incident, reinforcing the first. A year later, while conducting a Seminar in Missouri, a deeply religious individual asked, "What is the significance of the Commandment, 'Thou shalt not covet'?" Never having pondered that one before, I gave him what is a correct answer to many questions, "I do not know." However, the query kept nagging at me—a challenge that wouldn't down.

After considerable reflection, I realized that this Commandment—the tenth—is more important than all but the first. Covetousness—envy—lies at the root of stealing, killing, bearing false witness, and other evils. My conclusion: To the extent that the souls of Americans are cleansed of envy and covetousness, to that extent will we be graced with stalwart, righteous citizens. What's the formula for ridding ourselves of these traits? *Count our blessings!*

As related to this thesis, there is an attitude that dominates thinking and another that could become dominant. Voltaire expressed my views: "The longer we dwell on our misfortunes, the greater is their power to *harm* us."

Just as obvious: "The longer we dwell on our blessings, the greater is their power to *improve* us."

As to the first attitude, one should, by all means, be keenly aware of the misfortunes which beset society. Properly assessed, they are steppingstones to truth—blessings in disguise. Learn the wrong, to find the right!

Voltaire, however, had in mind the common attitude he observed in his time—two centuries ago—which is precisely what we observe in the U.S.A. today: citizens by the millions dwelling *only* on the countless misfortunes. The result of this myopic, unperceptive, shortsighted view? Ruled by pessimism, hopelessness, despair, such persons become crepehangers, doubting Thomases, worrywarts. Harm to themselves? The famous Dr. Charles Mayo wrote:

Worry affects the circulation—the heart, the glands, the whole nervous system. I have never known a man who died from overwork, but many who died from doubt.

These people not only do irreparable harm to their own lives but a disservice to the rest of us and, may I add, to the cause of human liberty. No truth was ever advanced by dwelling only on man-made misfortunes founded, as they are, on ignorance or untruths or outright lies!

Turn now from the negative to the positive, from dwelling on our misfortunes to dwelling on our blessings, from looking hellward to peering heavenward, from that which harms to that which improves. If enough of us do this our countrymen *"will know* what precious blessings they are in possession of, and which no other people on earth enjoy." Too high an aspiration? A bit of reflection will easily replace misery with joy, forlornness with hopefulness.

Conceded, no person will ever count all of his or her blessings. The human being does not exist who can count that far—our blessings border on the Infinite. Every heartbeat is a blessing, as is every breath, all discoveries, inventions, insights, intuitive flashes that have advanced truth and human welfare since the dawn of consciousness. So numerous, they stagger the imagination—delightfully!

Thomas Jefferson's reference was to the countless blessings Americans enjoy relative to people of other nationalities who lived at his time and before. Imagine, the greatest outburst of creative energy in all history, each individual, regardless of his or her station, free to act creatively; serfdom squelched, dictocrats unseated—the American miracle! My explanation of this phenomenon, with its unrecognized blessings galore, is in the third chapter of this volume. Jefferson had reason aplenty to lament the dearth of appreciation—this blindness to blessings—in his time. Were he among us today, what would his phrasing be? My guess: "Thank God! I can at least count my own blessings."

Well, in this respect, give America some more Jeffersons! Why is it that the more we dwell on our blessings, the greater is their power to improve us? There are more reasons than I shall ever know, but here are three:

- When the eye is cast on one's blessings, covetousness is overwhelmed; there remains no envy to darken the soul.
- Dwelling on our blessings aligns us with reality. Blessings, as heartbeats, are so commonplace that, short of conscious effort, they are not recognized. Counting them, day in and day out, impresses upon our minds how greatly they grace our lives and how relatively insignificant are our misfortunes.
- Individuals who are reaching for this truth are learning. By their own enlightened prescription, they are teachable. And as the Third Beatitude has it, "The teachable shall inherit the earth."[1]

What is meant by "earth" as here used? To repeat what I have written before, it has nothing to do with acres of diamonds, soil, rock. Rather, it relates to man's earthly

---

[1] For an explanation of the Third Beatitude and its meaning, see the chapter, "The Meek Shall Inherit the Earth," in my *Having My Way*, FEE, 1974, pp. 12-16.

potentialities: the evolution or emergence of individual faculties, a growth in awareness, perception, consciousness.

Stated another way, those who have so gained a control of themselves as to allow the search for Truth to take charge of their lives are the ones who have the capacity to live their earthly lives to the full: to them the real treasures of this mortal life belong.

To me, the Third Beatitude means: The teachable shall be graced with a realization of their potentialities. How do we become teachable? The simplest of all formulas: *Count our blessings!* Not only our numberless personal blessings but, as well, the blessings bestowed on us by Thomas Jefferson and others among America's Founding Fathers!

INDEX

Prepared by Vernelia A. Crawford

The letter "n" following a number indicates a footnote.

A

Abundance, 15
Adversity, 41-3
Agar, Herbert, 93
Americanism, 19, 105
Amiel, Henri-Frederic, 55, 135
Antagonist, 36
Aristotle, 125
Augustine (Saint), vii, 11, 23
Authoritarianism, 17-20; *see also*
  Government
Azzai, Simon Ben, 110

B

Basler, Roy P., 122n
Bastiat, Frederic, 84, 91
Beecher, Henry Ward, 119, 135
Behaviorism, 17-22, 106-107, 115-
  19, 125-30, 131

Benefactors, 96-8, 111
Bill of Rights, 17, 20-21, 31, 37
Blessings, 14, 17-44, 47-8, 144-8
Böhm-Bawerk, Eugen, 24-5
Bradford, Ralph, 72
Bright, John, 129
Browning, Robert, 42, 131
Bryant, William Cullen, 42
Bulwer-Lytton, Edward, vii
Burgess, John W., 39
Burke, Edmund, 15-16, 36
Businessmen, 110-14
Butler, Samuel, 97
Byron, George Gordon, 42

C

Cameron, Margaret, 73
Carlyle, Thomas, 108
Carson, Clarence, 71n
Channing, William Ellery, 43

Charity, 47, 120-24
Chesterton, G. K., 131
Choice-making, 25-6, 87-92
Christina, Queen of Sweden, 8, 16
Cobden, Richard, 129
Coercion, 21, 65-8, 83-5, 89
Collyer, Robert, vii
Command Society, 18, 25-6, 43-52, 96
Commandeer, 43, 45
Communication, 47-9, 58-62, 63-8
Communist Manifesto, 30, 40, 124
Competition, 47-8, 110-14
Confucius, 143
Conscience, 56
Consciousness, 24, 26, 121
Constitution, U.S., 17, 20-1, 37
Councils, 55-7
Counsels, 56-7
Covetousness, 14, 145
Cowper, William, 28
Creative energy
    foresight and, 96-8
    growth of, 37-8, 82, 90-2, 131-3
    opposition to, 28
    outburst of, 17, 114, 117-18

D

Declaration of Independence, 17, 31, 108-109, 129
Descartes, 8
Despotism, 22, 81-2
Destruction, agents of, 45-52
Dictocrats, 45-52, 64, 69-73, 83-5; *see also* Government
Differences, role of, 27-35
Domitian, 81-2, 84
Dreamers, 70-73

E

Economic calculation, 74-80
Economics defined, 21
Edison, Thomas Alva, 25, 99, 102
Education, 4-5, 32-3, 99-102, 125-30
Edwards, Tyron, 87
Egotism, 10
Emancipators, 108-14
Emerson, Ralph Waldo, vii, 5, 10, 12-13, 42, 135
Enlightenment, 3, 14, 21-2, 55, 108-14; *see also* Education
Epictetus, 25, 81-82
Erhard, Ludwig, 129
Error/Evil, 27-8, 40-43, 81-90, 93-8, 120-4

F

Faith, vii, 1-7, 14
Forecasting freedom, 1-7
Fosdick, Harry Emerson, 140
Foundation for Economic Education, 5, 30, 33, 37, 54, 71, 144
Founding Fathers, 17, 20-22, 113-14
Free market society
    businessmen in, 110-14
    dreamers in, 70-73
    economy of, 74-80
    miracles of, 17-22, 38, 48-52, 129
    types of, 45-52
    see also Freedom
Freedom
    charity and, 120-24
    choice-making and, 25-6, 87-92
    competition and, 47-8, 110-14

economy of, 74-80
education for, 4-5, 32-3, 99-102,
    125-30
faith in, vii, 1-7, 14
forecasting, 1-7
human, 136-7
leaders of, 15-22, 30-31, 108-109,
    113-14, 129-30
learning about, 4-5, 32-3, 125-30
nature of, 44
political, 37-9
responsibility for, 45, 89-91
slavery and, 81-6, 104-14, 137
value in, 28-35
Future, vision of, 2-3, 85

G

Giving, 17-22
Goethe, Johann Wolfgang, vii, 81,
    137
Government
    authoritarian, 17-20
    charity, 47, 120-24
    coercion and, 21, 65-8, 83-5, 89
    command of, 18, 25-6, 43-52, 96
    despotic, 22, 81-2
    dictatorship in, 45-52, 64, 69-73,
        83-5
    income, 39, 74-80, 124
    intervention, 21-2, 38
    limited, 17-22, 37-8, 75, 82
    monopoly, 47-8, 116-17
    planning, 95-8
    postal system of, 47-9
    power, 9, 20, 131
    socialistic. *See* Socialism
    statesmen of, 60
    statistics in, 74-80

subsidy, 68, 83
surrender to, 45
taxation by, 39, 124
Gross National Product, 74-5, 77-9
Growth, 74-80, 127

H

Habit, 27, 84
Hafed, 25
Haldane, John, 69
Hall, Verna, 45
Happiness, 23-4
Hayek, F. A., 95, 96n
Hazlitt, Henry, 6, 21, 36-7, 77, 83
    119, 126
Heathens, 61
Heber, Reginald, 61
Heritage, 17-22
Heroism, 134-8
Hocking, William E., 45-6
Hubbard, Elbert, 106
Hugo, Victor, 43
Humility, 10, 14, 139-43
Huxley, Aldous, 58-9, 62

I

Idle words, 58-62
Income, national, 39, 74-80, 124
Individualism, 8-16, 22, 27, 69-73
Inheritance, 17-22
Integrity, 4, 14, 34-5, 93, 139

J

James, William, 9-10
James I, v, 17

Jasper Karl, 127
Jefferson, Thomas, 129, 144, 146-48
Journal, preparation of, 12-16, 53

K

Kant, Immanuel, 118
Kettering, C. F., 56
Keynes, John Maynard, 90,
    116-17
Kleinknecht, C. F., 23
Knowledge, 4-5, 32-3, 99-102,
    125-30

L

Lawbreakers, 71
Leadership, 15-22, 30-31, 108-109,
    113-14, 129-30
Learning, 4-5, 32-3, 99-102, 125-30
Liberty, v, 17, 37; *see also*
    Freedom
Lincoln, Abraham, 120, 122-3
Longfellow, Henry W., 42

M

McBain, Hughston, 86
Mackay, Charles, 90n
Mail delivery, 47-9
Malice, 120-24; *see also* Error/Evil
Mallet, David, 42
Manion, Clarence, 25n
Maritain, Jacques, 63
Marx, Karl, 28, 70
Masses, 31-2, 95, 111, 134-8
Matthew V, 121n

Matthew VI, 61
Matthew VII, 102
Matthew XII, 58
Matthew XVIII, 139
Mayo, Charles, 146
Measurement, 74-80
Medicine men, 64-5
Menlo Park, 99
Mentality, 63-8
Methodology, 29-35
Mill, John Stuart, 22, 27
Millikan, Robert A., 41
Minding one's business, 24, 112
Miracles, 17-22, 38, 48-52, 129
Mises, Ludwig von, 6, 24, 33, 50,
    76, 129-30
Monopoly, 47-8, 116-17
Montaigne, Michel de, 112
Mosaic Law, 15
Mullendore, William, 4, 6

O

Opinions, 27-35, 58-62, 106
Organizations, 33-4
Ortega y Gasset, José, 134, 138
Ovid, 43

P

Pascal, Blaise, 24
Perfection, 8-16, 17-22
Philanthropy, 47, 120-24
Plunder, 21n, 84
Polarity, 41
Politics, 30, 37-38, 60
Postal system, 47-9
Prayer, 14

Pre-emptors, 45-52
Principles evaluated, 115-19
Problems
  blessings of, 14, 17-44, 47-8,
    144-8
  social, 102-107
Production, 50, 96
Progress, 36, 74-80, 115-19, 136
Promises, 93-8
Property, 122
Prosperity, 9, 15, 38, 74-80, 122-4

R

Rabelais, François, 1
Reason, 2, 56, 84
Responsibility, 45, 89-91
Right and wrong, 28, 106-107,
  115-19
Robertson, F. W., 125
Roepke, Wilhelm, 129
Rogers, Will, 126
Rogge, Benjamin, 115
Rothbard, Murray, 77
Russia, 91n

S

Scherman, Harry, 93
Self-analysis, 102-107, 139-43
Selfhood, 8-16
Shakespeare, William, 27, 31, 42
Silence, 62
Sixteenth Amendment, 39, 40
Slavery, 81-6, 104-107, 108-14, 137
Smith, Adam, 74, 85, 96
Smith, Sydney, 2

Socialism
  case against, 48-52
  definition of, 104-105
  economic calculating in, 77-8
  growth of, 3, 6, 36-7, 40, 43-4
  postal system and, 47-8
Society
  Command, 18, 25-6, 43-52, 96
  ideal, 69
  types of, 45-52
  see also Free market society
Socrates, 99
Spencer, Herbert, 83, 135-36
Statesmen, 60
Statistics, 74-80
Stealing, 88, 116-17
Subjective judgment, 79-80
Subsidy, 68, 83
Success, 36
Sumner, William Graham, 94-5, 98,
  111-12
Survival, 24-6

T

Taxation, 39, 124
Tennyson, Alfred, 2, 43
Theft, 88, 116-17
Tolerance, 27, 35
Tolstoy, Leo, 55, 56n
Truth
  direction of, 40-43
  error and, 27-8, 81
  humility and, 10, 14, 139-43
  integrity and, 4, 14, 34-5, 93, 139
  perceived, 10-11, 85-6

search for, 99-102, 127-8
Tylor, E. B., 74

V

Value judgments, 28-35, 53-7,
    79-80, 115-19
Vinci, Leonardo da, 49
Virtues
  charity as, 120-24
  evil and, 40-43
  humility as, 10, 14, 139-43
  integrity and, 4, 14, 34-35, 93, 139

tolerance as, 27, 35
Voltaire, 145

W

Wealth, 9, 15, 38, 74-80, 122-4
Whately, Richard, vii
White, Stewart Edward, 11, 127
Williams, Roger J., 91n
Wilson, Woodrow, 53, 55
Wonders, 131-33, 142; *see also*
    Blessings; Miracles